"The only one factor that I can positively link to the value of a currency, and I'm not really sure why, is the direct relationship with defense spending,"
Dennis Gartman, Publisher of The Gartman Letter and Fund Manager.

"I think that one will always make a lot of money by betting against the wisdom of central banks,"
Dennis Gartman, Publisher of The Gartman Letter and Fund Manager.

"I cannot stand the hypocrisy that circles the Royal Family, often disguised as criticism. The obsession with one family, as if they either were or ought to be miraculous if only they can behave better, is offensive to me as a rational being."
Sir Samuel Brittan, Assistant Editor, Financial Times of London

"The Monarchy was not much affected by the collapse of Barings, since most of the assets of the Royal family are in shares, trusts or land. They really only keep petty cash in the bank."
Sir Samuel Brittan, Assistant Editor, Financial Times of London

"The recent experience with respect to the pursuit of monetary policy from 1991 to 1993 was a repeat of the errors that the U.S. Federal Reserve made during the years of the 1930s great depression . . . This entire episode was repeated in the 1990s in Europe. Germany convinced most European Union members that inflation was about the only important policy goal to be concerned with."
Paul DeGrauwe, Member of the Belgian Senate

"I see very few attractions to Paris as the main financial centre. If the U.K. participates in a single European currency, there is no question of London remaining the pre-eminent financial centre."
Paul DeGrauwe, Member of the Belgian Senate

"Since 1978, the year that deregulation became official, an estimated 150 new airlines entered into the competitive game, of which 118 declared bankruptcy or merged with other carriers."
Sami Helewa, Jesuit and U.S. Aviation Commentator

"The lessons from the crisis in Mexico are threefold. Firstly, if you are going to have a devaluation, plan it properly. Secondly, have your people on side to talk to the New York bankers about the shift in the domestic economic policy framework, and lastly, don't go on vacation the week after you devalue."
Alan M. Rugman, Thames Water Professor of International Business, Oxford University.

"Americans are notoriously xenophobic. Only 15 percent of American citizens carry a passport. Which means 85 percent don't care much about anything outside of the U.S. There is not a leading community in the U.S. which understands international finance and economics,"
Alan M. Rugman, Thames Water Professor of International Business, Oxford University.

"To be a player internationally, you have to be in Asia. One amazing fact is how few American firms or European firms are competing with the Japanese. In short, Japan is leading world trade and investment which is why the yen is so strong."
Alan M. Rugman, Thames Water Professor of International Business, Oxford University.

"If the Bosnian crisis has shown anything, it is that U.S.-led NATO is the one serious organisation in Europe and any idea of a common EU foreign policy is still very far away,"
Chris Cviic, British Commentator,
Author and Journalist.

"Russia is currently going towards a rather chaotic period of privatisation and transformation. Its evolving into some form of corporatist state . . . with a great deal of flexibility through the element of organised crime."
Chris Cviic, British Commentator
Author and Journalist.

"George Soros has taken up a number of projects that could not have been financed by existing institutions."
Chris Cviic, British Commentator,
Author and Journalist.

"In recent years, we have incorporated several words in our modern language. Terms or euphemisms like globalization, competitiveness, total quality management, derecruitment and downsizing. All these personify in some form or another the "new" political and economic age we live in. The phrase "information superhighway" is a culmination of such thinking."
Jerry J. Khouri, Journalist and Middle East Consultant

". . . while the debate over the Tobin tax, derivatives, foreign exchange markets and other issues rage, traded markets will continue to innovate and grow. If roadblocks are put in their way the markets and the people will move."
Dr. John Pattison, Specialist in Compliance and Regulatory Affairs and Executive, CIBC World Markets

"The Bank of England is a good example of a balanced and cost effective regulatory regime as noted above. Singapore is also a good example. It is regrettable that the Barings episode occurred on their territory . . ."
Dr. John Pattison, Specialist in Compliance and Regulatory Affairs and Executive, CIBC World Markets

"The key structural change variable can be summed up in one word . . . "QUALITY." The Japanese introduced high quality vehicles into North America in the 1980's.
By the end of the 1980's virtually everyone had significantly increased their quality levels."
*Dennis DesRosiers, President,
DesRosiers Automotive Consultants*

"Overall, we look at our strategy of operation from a U.S. vantage point, as opposed to a Canadian, where our head office is located."
Richard Venn, Chairman and CEO, CIBC World Markets

"When an outsider from Japan receives subsidies in the U.K. to build a new plant, along with an opportunity to hire a young and well-trained workforce, something must be done in Brussels to level the playing field . . ."
Philippe H. Gras, Deputy General Director of Renault

"London is proving that you do not need to have a national industrial base in order to succeed in the financial services business. You can have a weak industrial base and a strong financial market culture. This will become even more pronounced, since the U.K.'s industrial base will become even weaker in the future, and the financial services side even stronger."
Laurent Tréca, Director General, Banexi (BNP)

"... as a general rule, the Deutsche mark and the Japanese yen do well in times of peace, but will be set aside if any real broad conflict were to erupt."
Tihomir Mikulic, Chairman and Director, Kapital Trade

"... the U.S. was always inefficiently organised through massive government defense subsidies to whatever industry they decided to champion."
Tihomir Mikulic, Chairman and Director, Kapital Trade

"There is about $380 billion in real American currency circulating worldwide, and experts say there is at least $10 billion in bogus bills along for the ride. Of that $380 billion U.S. in currency, two-thirds of it circulates overseas- making the detection and confiscation of counterfeits difficult."
B.J. Del Conte, T.V. News Producer and Journalist

"The best regulatory model, and the one that follows simplicity the best is that of the U.K."
Dr. John Pattison, Specialist in Compliance and Regulatory Affairs and Executive, CIBC World Markets

G•7 Books
Published by The G•7 Report Inc.
The G•7 Report Inc., P.O. Box 824, Postal Stn. Q
Toronto, Ontario, M4T-2N7, Canada
E-mail: g7report@passport.ca; tel: 416 699 3530; fax: 416 699 5683

G•7 Books Registered Offices:
Toronto, Ontario, Canada

Printed and Manufactured in Belarus
by: World Wide Printing, 114 Wemborough Road, London, HA7 2EG, UK. Offices in
Minsk, Belarus and Duncanville, Texas, U.S.A.

National Library of Canada Cataloguing in Publication Data

Vukson, William B.Z., 1962-
From the collapse of the Cold War to the rise of the hot high tech wars

Rev. ed. Includes Index.
ISBN 1-894611-02-0

1. Economic history--1990- 2. International finance. 3. Globalization
I. Title.

HC59.15.V85 2001   330.9'049   C2001-900217-3

Visit the G•7 Group's website: www.G7Report.com

Illustration and design by Judy Willemsma, Toronto, Canada

Distributors: Orca Book Services, Stanley House, 3 Fleets Lane, Poole, Dorset, BH15
3AJ, UK. Send all orders via tel: 00 44 (0) 1202 665432; fax: 00 44 (0) 1202 666219
Email: orders@orcabookservices.co.uk

Global Marketing Representatives: Drake International Services Ltd., Market House,
Market Place, Deddington, Oxford, OX15 0SE, UK. tel: 00 44 (0) 1869 338240;
fax: 00 44 (0) 1869 338310; Email: info@drakeint.co.uk

THE **COLLAPSE**
HE **COLD WAR**
IE **RISE** OF THE
HOT HIGH **TECH WARS**

William B. Z. Vukson

A Business Reference for the "New Economy"

The Globalization Revolution

OTHER BOOKS IN THIS SERIES

Political, Structural and Technological Change

Three Investment Stories under Free Trade: Portfolio, Direct and Cross Border M&A

Emerging Markets & Special Surveys

Organized Crime and Money Laundering

William B. Z. Vukson

William B.Z. Vukson was born on June 24, 1962 in Toronto, Canada. He is the founding Publisher and Editor of The G•7 Report Inc., established in 1991, consisting of ten Special Information Publications on global investment risk and the Investors' Newsmagazine available over the retail newstrade in Canada and the United States. Mr. Vukson is also a Merchant Banker specialised in Central Europe and founder of a group of wholesale investment funds called G7Funds.

Mr. Vukson has obtained a B.A. in economics from the University of Toronto, Toronto, Canada, and an M.A. in economics from the Centre for Economic Studies, University of Leuven, Leuven, Belgium.

CREDITS

As the Chairman, Publisher and Editor of The G•7 Report Project, I would like to thank my Editors: Sami E. Helewa S.J., Jerry J. Khouri, Antonio Nicaso and Dennis DesRosiers; our specialist commentators: Dr. John C. Pattison, Francesco Riondino, Lee Lamothe, Tihomir Mikulic, Dr. Alan Rugman, Andreas Utermann, Paul Nielsen, Dr. Paul De Grauwe, Alex Constandse Dr. Michele Fratianni, and our internet site Webmaster: Marshall Heaton. Finally, I would like to thank Ms. Judy Willemsma, one of the most efficient Creative Directors that I have ever had the pleasure to work with.

I would also like to thank Andy J. Wood, Jean-Pierre Paelinck, Terry Labelle, George Valenta, Raymond Low, George Vukelich, Marinko Papuga, Al Petrie, Johan Lambrecht, Chris Cviic, Jayson Myers, Mark Chandler, James Farmer, Mark A.A. Warner, Frank Boll, Douglas W. J. Young, Ron Dodds, Joanne Girouard, Giovanni Giarrusso and all others that were involved with this project over the past years.

William B.Z. Vukson

Table of Contents

PREFACE

This book is related to four other books *(I: Political, Structural and Technological Change; II: THREE INVESTMENT STORIES UNDER FREE TRADE: Portfolio, Direct and Cross Border M&A; III: Emerging Markets and Special Surveys; IV: Organised Crime and Money Laundering)* and was authored or edited by William B.Z. Vukson throughout June and July of 2000. It is a concise overview of some of the most important recent geo-political and economic developments affecting global commercial strategies, and laying the groundwork for the understanding of the revolutionary decade of globalisation; the "1990s." The focal point for this overview more or less begins in the turbulent 1970s, under a time when OPEC, the Red Brigades and the European Monetary System negotiated by Helmut Schmidt and Valéry Giscard d'Estaing were all evolving. In essence, an attempt is made to account for the revolutionary nature of the 1990s by using the turbulent 1970s as a loose benchmark throughout.

The related series of books referred to above in *italics*, are a collection of articles and interviews that began in January of 1992 and continued until December of 1999, published in *The G•7 Report: Investors' Newsmagazine*. It is an historical and eyewitness account of the period by an eclectic group of writers and contributors. It can be called an "anthology" of the 1990s and a witness to this period of globalisation. Although some articles are five years or older, readers may be surprised to find how relevant the issues are as they have been presented, even today as we begin to progress through the new millennium. Many of the articles and interviews capture the essence of change and help in identifying vital trends and geo-strategic patterns. The policy of *The G•7 Report* and its editors and contributors has always been one of objectivity and neutrality. Many differing viewpoints were encouraged, although readers may get the impression at times, that there was an over-reliance on market solutions to problems raised by the rapid globalisation of markets and technological change.

Although allocation and distribution of income are now determined by a global market more than at any time in recent history, the road ahead may not be so clear. Just as the experiment with unfettered markets collapsed at the end of the nineteenth century, so too may our current globalised market system become transformed in the future. To understand the direction of this future can only begin by examining in great detail the decade of the 1990s.

The G•7 Report Project

THE
GLOBALIZATION
REVOLUTION

FOREWORD

The G•7 Report Project came about unexpectedly. After having spent many years in academia, trade and merchant banking, I felt that a new communications forum was needed that would bind together an inter-disciplinary approach to the new developments and challenges faced in this emerging new decade, the 1990s. As things turned out, the past decade proved to be one of the most revolutionary periods in the twentieth century, with an unprecedented combination of global markets and technological invention. All of this called for a fresh new start in media, research and documentary journalism that yearned for direction from a unique type of leader; perhaps one that brought to the table a rare combination of both academic and theoretical grounding, combined with unequalled practical know-how. To be an effective leader or strategist in the 1990s, it was not enough to just be a specialist within a narrow area of expertise, nor was it sufficient to rely on just many years of "experience" within a particular sector of the economy.

In this respect, the academic approach to economics and world business was deprived of what John Kenneth Galbraith once termed as "practical good sense" evident in great abundance throughout the revolutionary 1990s. Even within the confines of the "new high tech economy" a great deal is lost in trying to understand the longer term trends that are in play, let alone in predicting the rise and progress of this new high tech world. Very few Economists in the early years of this decade predicted what has transpired via the internet, nor has the profession been too adept at charting the long term trends that have been emerging in global stock markets, not to mention the currency markets. In fact, on the latter point, most have dismissed trends in currency markets as belonging within the sphere of the random walk. Asked where the dollar-yen parity may be tomorrow or one month from now, the quick reply would have been "the same as where the relationship has stood at the close of business today." Asked where it would stand one or two years from today, the answer would amazingly have been the same. Yes, the new orthodoxy in the 1990s was the random walk. Under this method of analysing currency markets, there was no way to predict the short term daily or hourly parities between two currencies, nor was there any strategy to pursue long term risk management of fluctuating currencies.

The name, "The G•7 Report," was derived from an international monetary economics course that I attended and which was taught by Professor Michele Fratianni, an expert on exchange rates and interest rates and former Chief Economist of the European Commission in Brussels and a member of the Council of Economic Advisors in Ronald Reagan's Administration, not to mention a good friend of mine. Of interest was how both fiscal and monetary policy was formulated within the industrial grouping of the most powerful economies in the world, the interaction between them, and the effects a particular direction would have on the emerging market group of countries that border these powerful G•7 nations.

In simple English, if all of the members of the G•7 were expanding fiscal spending or lowering interest rates in concert with one another, the disruption as reflected via fluctuating exchange rates would be kept to a minimum. This would be of particular benefit to all parties transacting international business, since strategy and planning within organisations find it most difficult to hedge the effects of gyrating exchange rates. On many occasions, the serious financial press is full of reports of disappointing earnings results due to financial hazards that have impacted subsidiaries in various parts of the world.

The initial attempts to co-ordinate official demand-creation activities within the G•7 have been motivated to a large extent on purely trade grounds. Liberalised capital mobility and the burgeoning "herd-mentality" lead by some well known hedge-funds is a phenomenon that arose in the early 1990s, through George Soros' glorious victory in ejecting the pound sterling out of the European Exchange Rate Mechanism, which was the prelude to the present day single currency- the Euro. However, in the mid 1980s, the hey-day of G•7 policy co-ordination exercises, it was trade concerns which were at the forefront of the policy debates.

After Francois Mitterrand's Socialist Party took power in 1981, politicians in France broke with their G•7 counter-parts in order to pursue a massive re-inflation which ultimately proved very short-lived. To break from the pack in such a manner, the French franc nose-dived in global currency markets as inflation skyrocketed upwards. The Mitterrand government quickly learned that individualistic approaches to policy were dead ends, and that the short-lived expansion quickly made the exchange rate attractive to foreign buyers, but that the ensuing price increases, or inflation, choked off the gains that buyers would have had from the lower franc. In short, the "Mitterrand experiment" exacted great inefficiencies on fellow member G•7 nations and had limited real impacts on the domestic French economy. Mitterrand quickly retreated from this approach and agreed to become a team player thereafter.

Not only were such policy directions between the world's most powerful economies vital in understanding how business cycles interact between these countries, but a collective decision to increase spending or to lower interest rates exacted a real impact on the global economy, and the emerging market countries in particular. During the transformation of Russia and the former communist countries of central and eastern Europe, many have argued in favour of a concerted G•7 expansion in spending and their creation of a more global demand that would in turn assist in the transformation to a market system. This criticism remains valid as trade and investment flows from the G•7 to the newly emerging market economies and vice-versa, has been disappointing, hence prolonging the transformation process and creating more hardship than what would have been otherwise necessary.

The G•7 Report project was not just about economics and business, but was a new vehicle that introduced a number of journalists and commentators unfamiliar to the readers of the daily news in major North American cities. We retained some leading contributors over the years, such as Harvard Professor Benjamin Friedman, Belgian Senator and leading international trade Economist Paul De Grauwe and compliance and regulatory expert Dr. John Pattison, but also introduced numerous writers that would normally not have had the opportunity in the commercialised or market-driven media to express their views and communicate with our readers. We became known as a media that was made available to some leading European based journalists such as Italian based organised crime expert, Antonio Nicaso, and to his counterpart in Canada, Mr. Lee Lamothe, the former head of the crime section of the Toronto Sun daily newspaper.

The G•7 Report project attained a small "niche" circulation in major North American cities such as New York, Boston, Miami, San Francisco, Los Angeles, Toronto and Montreal, but was never able to develop a following in places such as Vancouver or Atlanta. Moreover, throughout 1995 and 1996 we were also available over the retail newstrade in the City of London at selective newsagents. Furthermore, The G•7 Report project was not something that was developed by marketers residing in New York, Toronto or Los Angeles. In fact, I would be the first to stick my neck out and say that this was among very few recent launches which went the other way around. I did not "measure" or "test" the market with this concept before launching the product. In essence, The G•7 Report made and shaped its own following and market over the years. It was a leader which was embraced by a very loyal grouping of reader, that felt that we had important things to say about global trends and the rising "new economy."

The G•7 Report project was particularly foreign to advertisers, especially among the agencies in Toronto. We counted very limited success in soliciting advertising support, and agency calls and presentations tended to border on the absurd. In short, The G•7 Report was simply not a concept that was welcomed within this realm. Most of the major corporate supporters were much appreciated, yet very rare. Among this select group, we are very grateful to

Ford Motor Company, the Montreal Stock Exchange, NatWest Markets and Kapital Trade as our core group of advertisers. The problem that any "niche" publisher must go through is retaining a core group of supporters over the long term. If this can not be maintained, then the publication either dies or gets transformed over the years. We greatly relied on the latter technique to ensure our survival. However, it was interesting to note that we did not deviate much from our core group of readers, regardless of the format of The G•7 Report. Since 1992, we went from an academic-looking journal to an expensive full-glossy magazine, to a newsprint version and ending with the current newsletter look. We found that the constant throughout this entire process of transformation in design were our core readers over the years, and for this we thank them for their ongoing and unbending support.

William B.Z. Vukson

A SNAPSHOT OF THE TRANSITION TO GLOBALISATION

As the US economy emerged from the 1970s oil shock, a consensus was building that inflation was one of the western world's worst enemies. The ineptitude of the Carter Administration's inability to manage the domestic economy culminated in the bungled Iran hostage rescue mission. Meanwhile on the other side of the Atlantic, UK voters just elected a refreshing new politician, which was not merely a break from the string of familiar Labour governments throughout the 1970s, but whose leader was a woman. In a symbolic move, Margaret Thatcher immediately asserted her authority by confronting a violent miners strike and doing the unthinkable, by imprisoning their leader, Sir Arthur Scargill. This one symbolic act tended to revolutionise Great Britain throughout the 1980s, as the Thatcher government moved very quickly to maintain the market friendly momentum that had built up from the election, and privatise the symbols of Labour governments gone by.

Meanwhile, the election of Ronald Reagan and the Republicans in 1980 co-incided with the Carter Administration appointment of Paul Volcker as the new Chairman of the Federal Reserve Board, replacing Arthur Burns. Volcker's move to quickly assert monetary target management caused a record run-up in short term interest rates, that nearly crossed over into the twenty percent range. The changing face of policy within this anglo grouping of countries was in contrast to the continuation of the Cold War system of relations between nation-state blocs. The Cold War was one common feature that continued to pre-occupy policy-makers, in terms of the enormous budgetary commitments and outlays, that were needed to periodically fund the massive missile pro-grams approved by the Pentagon.

The Reagan Administration moved to heighten the anxiety of European coun-tries that bordered the Soviet bloc even further, by first suggesting that a "limit-ed tactical" nuclear war was winnable, and then that the US would be inclined towards building a new line of defensive weapons that adopted the popular theme of "Star Wars." Furthermore, his Administration moved to dramatically increase the real expenditures on new arms initiatives, that proved to be very difficult for the Kremlin to match dollar for dollar.

Meanwhile, early evidence of technological change was detected in the 1980s, as the banking sector began to introduce new "NOW" chequing accounts, that carried a higher rate of interest than what was available on traditional savings accounts. A first sign that the new regime of monetary targeting under Paul Volcker, would prove to be far more difficult than what was originally envi-sioned. Also, the complete collapse in stock market prices throughout the infla-tionary 1970s, began to come alive once again in the 1980s, as new leveraged financing and debt management techniques were mobilised to serve sharehold-ers. Although corporations had very little debt as part of their capital base in the 1970s, their share prices were, almost paradoxically, permanently depressed. The relationship between no or very little debt and share prices was almost non-existent. However, when these same companies opted to take on more leverage in the 1980s, or when a hostile takeover was launched via a leveraged buy-out, their share prices rose as less stock was outstanding and more and more companies were engaged in the process of buying back their shares. Therefore, there was an optimal debt to equity ratio that was engineered throughout the mid to latter half of the 1980s, which played a very big role in breathing some life back into the Dow Jones Industrial Average.

Technology was beginning to make life difficult for the Federal Reserve, just as Alan Greenspan was enticed from his private consulting practice in New York to head up the central bank in 1987. Gone were the years when strict mone-tarism or the targeting of M1, M2 and M3 was possible. Now, there began a proliferation of financial innovations in savings and deposit accounts, which made the measurement of simple monetary base extremely difficult. Gone were any direct links between the M-measurements and inflation, and central banks began to concentrate more on targeting just the inflation rate. Such developments were not only playing havoc with domestic institutions and the drafting of policy, but were also beginning to change the face of the Cold War system. The rise of Perestroika in the Soviet Union and the move to appoint a more modern leader in the form of Mikhail Gorbachev, opened up many new avenues of communication within the Soviet bloc countries. Once the eventual collapse of the Berlin Wall came, it initiated a domino effect in the region that surprised even the most seasoned experts and commentators. The new decade of the 1990s came in with a bang, and the revolutionary change that began this great transformation continues today. Economic and business life after the Cold War, is barely distinguishable with what were the common norms in the 1980s. These differences can best be illustrated through a simple economic and business relationship that defines the composition of a typical G•7 country (U.S., Canada, Germany, France, Italy, Japan, U.K.).

In each component of demand that determines the make up and the expansion of a country's total production of goods and services or Gross National Product (GNP), the difference in the nature of each decade of the 1980s and the 1990s can be compared. In its simple format, the demand that drives all business decisions in any country, hence creating the GNP, can be represented via the following relationship: "$y = c + i + g + ex - im$", where "c" stands for consumer spending- a very big component in most G•7 economies where it represents some two-thirds of both of Japan and the U.S. total production of goods and services. The "i" represents investment in productive assets; "g" represents government expenditures; "ex" represents exported goods and services to other countries, while "im" is the converse, and represents imported goods and services into a given country.

In this simple relationship, we can look at the nature of each component that determines production before and after the collapse of the Cold War system. If we concentrate on consumer spending or the "c," we can state that it was much more difficult to be a consumer during the Cold War, since goods and services were more prone to inflation, and there was not as much abundance in consumer choice relative to the 1990s. Also, the full effects of technology were not being felt in the 1980s; there did not yet exist the entire concept of e-commerce, where consumers could surf the internet and compare prices and "deals" on items ranging from telephone rates to kitchen appliances. Further, the military-industrial complex of the Cold War was in its heyday throughout the 1980s, as Ronald Reagan's arms build-up naturally diverted resources away from their alternative uses, which for our purposes could be defined in the form of consumer products and services.

Investment spending or the "i" component in our simple equation underwent a profound change throughout this period of transformation that culminated in the system of "globalisation." Investment spending within the G•7 group of countries in the 1980s was driven by the arms race, that was initiated by the Reagan Administration, and supported by Congress and the government of Margaret Thatcher in the UK. The entire G•7 was engaged in this military build-up, as tax cuts in both the U.S. and the UK, served to raise budget deficits and "crowd-out" all investment spending that did not originate at the Pentagon in Washington D.C. Private investment spending on plant and equipment that did not originate from the Pentagon had a very difficult time. The unprecedented tax cuts and growing deficits in the U.S. brought with them a rising real rate of interest, that made non-Pentagon originated projects extremely difficult to finance profitably. The only sector that saw a boom during this period was property development, but this does not make up a component of investment spending or "i."

The decade of the 1990s brought about both a technological and financial revolution that combined to advance the development of each other. In fact, technology to now has had its greatest impact on banking and finance. The 1990s became the decade of venture capital, spurned by the enormous returns that were being made potentially available in high tech and internet investments. Never before, during the Cold War system, has the U.S. financial system been so open and liberal in financing ideas. Many of the high technology investments being made in the latter half of the 1990s, were being financed as pure equity investments. This was also very different from the high deficit and high real interest rate era of the 1980s, as the high tech sector of the 1990s managed to escape any adverse effects from the "crowding-out" effect that normally associated debt and bank-financed investment projects. Therefore, the difference in the component of "i" was a very profound one within these two decades.

Taking into consideration government spending or "g," the Cold War was associated with very high deficits, as governments within the G•7 all pursued deficit financing to meet both military and social programs. Alongside the arms race, were commitments that were made to social programs by all countries. Furthermore, the collection of taxes was more difficult in the 1980s, as levies on goods are far less lucrative than capital gains taxes on the steadily growing stock market turnover that became a feature of the 1990s. On the spending side, the 1990s or the post Cold War decade, was more concerned about pension and healthcare reforms, along with a real decline in military procurement. All of the European countries in the G•7 grouping, must address their aging populations in terms of how they fund their pension plans. Most countries operate under a "pay-as-you-go" system, where younger generations fund those that are retired. The transformation being encouraged by governments in these countries, would take the pension liability off of their budgets and would require private individuals to take up their own cause for their retirement years. Therefore, the last vestiges of the old Cold War system of "pay-as-you-go" pension systems, is under severe attack due to the aging population base. In short, expenditures and the activity of the "g" have become severely retrenched in the decade after the Cold War.

On the tax collection side, the 1990s have produced a nice windfall for most members of the G•7. The high technology that has combined with financial innovation, together with a rising equity market culture have all produced benefits for government budgets. The record rise in stocks in the latter half of the 1990s, has produced enormous revenues that have been almost effortlessly collected, due to the fact that they were capital gains levies on financial instruments, such as stocks and bonds. This phenomenon was led by the US, where evidence of a budget surplus was first detected in the mid 1990s, and spread to other members of the G•7, including continental European countries, co-inciding with the general upward shift in equity prices.

The trade balance of each country reflected through the "ex" component of our economic relationship, remained more or less consistent between the two decades. The U.S., both now and in the 1980s, struggles with a trade balance deficit as imports of luxury brand items from both Japan and Europe continue to exert pressures on the dollar. In the decade of the 1980s, it was the rising trade deficit with Japanese automotive exporters than created the conditions whereby the yen and Deutsche mark were revalued relative to the U.S. Dollar. However, the persistence of the trade deficit in the 1990s, has ironically co-incided with the opposite effects in the currency markets. Unlike the devaluation in the 1980s of the U.S. Dollar, the decade after the collapse of the Cold War is witness to a stronger currency. As the decade progressed, the U.S. Dollar only increased in value relative to the European blocs and sterling. The trade balance of continental European countries, by contrast, was always considered to be healthy if in surplus. Countries such as France, always expressed a preference for a surplus in their trade accounts, while Germany also was more often than not in a state of surplus. In the case of Italy, a surplus was also expected. The country that is known for exporting its luxury, fashions and lifestyle products to the world is usually in a position of surplus. The Europeans always considered a surplus to be a policy goal that industry should comply with.

In the case of the UK, the 1990s have brought with them an interesting twist in the tale of what has been on-going in their international accounts. The participation in the Exchange Rate Mechanism (E.R.M.) and the tacit acceptance of having sterling track the movement of the Deutsche Mark in the late 1980s, brought great pressures on its traditional manufacturing base. However, a consensus has been building for a very long time, that the service sector has gained prominence as a driver of G.N.P. to levels far in excess of the traditional manufacturing base. In short, manufacturers have seen a steady deterioration in not only their share of overall output in the U.K. economy, but also their political power is not what it once was. Having understood the decline in the relative importance of manufacturing, policy makers thought it alright to pursue service sector friendly policies, without much consideration of the effects on the external traded accounts.

Once sterling reached over-inflated levels both under the E.R.M. and more recently, after the launch of the new single European currency; the Euro, the Bank of England's panel of decision makers, continued to reject a reduction in base rates, in the belief that the inflation rate might edge up. The over-valued level of the currency did not gain the attention that the domestic rate of inflation had, leaving the British manufacturing industry pitted against the policy of the central bank. More and more, the new economy and high tech way of doing things have made the trade accounts less important to a number of countries. The U.K. may be a special case, but once the service sector and internet economies grow to a level of critical mass, the trade balance and the export of goods will become less and less relevant, as will the use of the currency in order to gain competitive export advantage in trade. Therefore, one thing that can be said about the "ex" component, is that it certainly does not play a role as important as it once held prior to the collapse of the Cold War political economy. The more that G•7 countries turn to the service sector as the major driver in their economies, the less will the export of goods be relevant. This development is already in place in the U.K. economy, but will be expected to lag among the continental G•7 countries.

The "im" or import component of the overall relationship is to a great extent similar in analysis to that afforded to "ex" or export component above, except that countries with a large deficit within a sector have been successfully persuading leading multinationals to establish a productive presence within their own jurisdictions, rather than continuing to run the growing deficit in trade. Very evident has been the activity on the part of U.K. based manufacturers, after clamouring to escape the harsh effects of sterling. Continental European countries, as well as certain sectors in the U.S., have been successful in substituting a direct investment commitment from them, instead of continuing to run the trade deficit. This "substitution effect" would not have been evident during the Cold War days as it is now. The liberalisation of the three forms of investment; portfolio, direct and cross border mergers and acquisitions, have also revolutionised the trade accounts among G•7 countries. When one country finds that a sector is in deficit, it moves to entice the exporting industries from the source country to set up an operation in the domestic market.

The simple business activity relationship: $y = c + i + g + ex - im$, is able to account for the differing nature of each component driving the production of goods and services when moving from the political economic system of the Cold War, to its ultimate collapse and the aftermath of globalisation. The "big picture" that is created by this simple relationship then leads to several stylised features of the systems, both past and present. The main facts can be summarised in the following terms:

Inflation

Inflation will not continue to predominate the new and more competitive consumer-driven era, as it has for most of the Cold War period.

News and Media

News and media and the overall coverage of issues and current events will continue to move away from black and white; us vs. them or good vs. bad, politically based issues to a more socially inspired view of the world. Noticeable throughout the 1990s, has been prime-time coverage or "CNNisation" of such noted melodramas as the O.J. Simpson Trial, Monica Lewinsky and Elian Gonzalez capers. This, in contrast to the 1980s pre-occupation with the spread of communism and the fearful spread of the weapons of mass destruction.

Corporate Culture

Countries and Corporations will become less distinguishable in terms of economic power and the drafting of policy. In order to attract the global pool of capital that can now freely be invested in any part of the world, countries will increasingly try to manage their budgetary affairs in the same fashion as modern corporations try to maximise their shareholder values. Increasingly evident will be initiatives to cut back social commitments to pensioners as well as welfare recipients, as politicians increasingly assume the role of efficient managers.

Branding

Countries or national governments will increasingly be in direct competition with some of the best run global corporations or name brands. Witness Microsoft Corporation's beligerance against what it perceives as the unjust meddling in its business affairs by the U.S. Federal Trade Commission in recommending a break-up of its monopoly position. Financial products issued by governments will increasingly be judged by portfolio managers in direct competition with the blue-chip stocks of I.B.M., General Electric, Citigroup and Wal-Mart.

Political Parties

Political decision making will be indistinguishable between right and left wing parties in each of the G•7 group, as will the commercial policies of each of the G•7. Globalisation and international capital mobility will effectively work to handcuff those politicians or parties that are considered hostile to the ideals of the free markets and monopoly capital.

M.B.A. Effect

There will be an even greater standardisation in the Global Management Culture evident in major Fortune 1000 corporations. This standard management culture will be promoted via "standardised and accredited" M.B.A. schools around the world, and will produce candidates that will be barely distinguishable in thought and mannerism from one another.

Financial City States

Competition between nation states will be increasingly replaced with competition between cosmopolitan Financial City States. New York, Toronto, London, Frankfurt and Tokyo will be the trend setters in the new global paradigm, as capital mobility will continue to eclipse international trade patterns of goods and services between nation-states and financial services will explode.

Excise and Customs Diplomacy

Diplomacy and International Politicking will be reduced to a trade and investment agenda, where issues arising from Customs and Excise matters will be the main outlines for negotiation.

Central Banking

Consolidation of independent central banks will spread from the experiment founded within the G•7 onwards to unsuspecting emerging market economies. More or less, the simultaneity of the technological revolution throughout the latter half of the 1990s and the withdrawal of active fiscal policy management, have created an environment where the dangers of inflation have been turned into the menace of disinflation and too much competition. The question that is foremost on the minds of decision makers is: Did central banks need that level of independence when technological advances were such a natural hedge against the risks of inflation in the first place?

Investment Philosophy

"Top-down" or the "Big Picture" approach to investing employed by the most successful hedge funds, has recently come under attack. The most famous global money manager, George Soros, is on record as saying that fundamentals are no longer feasible in an era of accelerating capital and investment flows. Capital flows will continue to eclipse trade-originated flows, and will move even further towards a mixed bag defined by portfolio, direct and cross border mergers and acquisitions. These will be determined by the risk-free rate differentials, as well as cross border mergers and acquisitions and the newly-discovered thirst for international blue-chip equities. The interaction of all of these flows will ultimately determine the direction of exchange rates and even interest rates.

ECONOMICS IN TROUBLE:
The Rise of Literature

The transition from one system in the 1980s to the post-Cold War globalisation, followed by the explosion in high tech, literally made the entire mode of analysis used by the financial analysis and economics professions redundant. When I look at the "top-heavy" faculties across North America, I often wonder what relevance there still exists between a professor that has successfully defended his or her doctoral thesis in the 1980s, let alone in the two decades prior to this. Many Economics Departments have not been very active in hiring new talent throughout the 1980s, hence most staff members can still be labeled as barely relevant dinosaurs hired on during the height of the Cold War.

In fact, I would not be surprised if one could not find more than one percent of the entire active professorial staff, who had the practical good judgement to successfully forecast the ending of the Cold War and what has transpired throughout the 1990s. Most of the profession involved in forecasting financial variables such as interest rates or exchange rates, have never been able to get it right. So much so, that in the late 1980s, they collectively called it a truce by resorting to the "random walk" theory in predicting where currency parities would be over the next day, week or month. The problem, is that most forecasters use historical data to extrapolate or extend their forecasts to future days, months and years. This is alright if all institutional or "structural" conditions continue to be the same, or hold constant. This certainly was not the story of the 1990s, as even a seasoned practitioner such as Federal Reserve Chairman Alan Greenspan, admitted that U.S. productivity numbers were very unusual and quite different from the historical norms, demanding an overhaul of the Fed decision-making apparatus.

As most of these economics faculties grapple with formal forecasts, they would be far better off to inject a little historical and literary analysis, coupled with practical good sense and "gut feel." This is the only way, in the modern and fast changing high tech world, that economists could continue to hold on to the small amount of credibility that they may have. When one tries to think of economic practitioners today that are relevant to the fast changing world, and to whom people sit up and listen to, only a rare few could be numbered on the fingers of one hand. Alan Greenspan is the pre-eminent "celebrity economist," but he has moved through the ranks the hard way. Having been in private consulting practice for many years, he was appointed to the main job at the Fed, after creating a reputation in Washington D.C., as President Gerald Ford's Chief Economic Advisor. Another name that comes to mind is that of John Kenneth Galbraith. Although a notable Professor at Harvard for many decades, Galbraith served as Ambassador to India during John F. Kennedy's Administration and was involved in several Commissions during the post War and depression era of the 1930s. Moreover, he authored several prolific books on welfare, including "The Culture of Contentment" in the early 1990s.

Some of the more influential academic economists include Robert Barro and Robert Lucas, who were instrumental in creating the "Rational Expectations" theory, which basically asserted the view that both fiscal and monetary policies had no effect on the real side of the economy or unemployment. This was developed, refined and used by others throughout the 1980s, such as Thomas Sargent of the University of Minnesota, to effectively reduce the involvement of government spending and participation in the economies' of G•7 countries.

It was also in many ways a framework that was established for Ronald Reagan's "supply-side" economics of the 1980s, and also the constitution which came to govern all central banks in the G•7. More specifically, by advancing the notion that monetary expansions that are not expected, can have an impact by increasing demand, hence incomes; by contrast those that are expected can have no real effect except on prices, hence creating inflation.

The extreme case has monetary policy directly linked to only the inflation rate. This is a model that is used by the Bank of England and only partially by the Federal Reserve. Note that the Fed has in many ways a contradictory mandate, which is to pursue maximum growth under conditions of stable prices. This was not possible under the confines of the old Cold War system, but is now evidently achievable in the new "high tech" world, as productivity growth continues to outstrip the historical long term natural growth trend in the U.S. under evidence of falling or stable prices.

Although these academic economists have made contributions, one often wonders if the natural progress of technology would have exerted deflationary effects anyway; without having to re-orient the constitution of central banks that emphasised targeting only inflation. The rapid growth of the internet has made conditions ultra-competitive for producers of similar products and services. Now, consumers and businesses can compare price lists in a matter of a few minutes and channel their procurement accordingly. This is a natural hedge against inflation, despite a resurgence in oil prices. Certainly, in a period of deflation in the 1990s, the model proposed for central banks has been made redundant. There has been an explosion of easy money, with skyrocketing money supplies that are beginning to have some effects in fueling the venture capital and private equity booms, hence impacting the real economy directly. These developments, flip the entire "Rational Expectations" theories concocted in the inflationary 1980s, right on their head.

One of the main goals of *The G•7 Report* project, was to avoid heavy theories and to engage economics as a general map, in order to guide the development of our forecasts and commentaries throughout the 1990s. Although many contributors were economists, and some were academic economists, we purposely tried to invite only the ones that we felt had a unique feel for the cross-disciplinary approach that was demanded during such a revolutionary period. The ideal type of commentator throughout this turbulent period would have been a cross between Greenspan, Galbraith and Lucas.

THE FED AND THE BUNDESBANK

Central banks have evolved from a monetary tool used at the will of governments throughout the 1960s to the 1980s, into an institution that was revered in the 1990s as the keeper of sound money and regulatory practice. Most G•7 countries have experienced direct subjugation of their central banks over the three decades prior to the 1990s, in one form or another. The two extreme cases were evident in both France and Italy, as the Banque de France and the Banca Italia, were mere extensions of the Treasury throughout this period. Having been placed in such a quagmire, they were notorious for having the wills of overly ambitious politicians continuously interfere with their mandates. Monetary policy was a tool that was used liberally during this period by both the Banque de France and Banca Italia, through their proxies, the respective Treasury Departments in both countries.

Whenever there was a need to supplement budgets, governments just issued bonds to their respective central banks and expanded the money supply, which usually led to hyper-inflation. The poor Italian southern region was continually appeased by such policies, as massive transfers were injected to develop various projects financed by huge state industrial conglomerates such as Iri. Whether or not the projects meant anything or were successful, was besides the point. The important thing was that any revenue shortfalls in the central budget, need not have been a major concern as tax evasion was rampant throughout the entire country. The important point was that the Banca Italia was called on to print more money in order to appease the politicians of the south, and to engage the workforce in some sort of activity.

Likewise, in the case of France, the governments of the 1960s and early 1970s, were well known for their use of the Banque de France money printing machine. Only in the mid 1980s, did France make a real effort to inject some sort of order in her monetary affairs by tying the franc to the German mark, hence buying credibility to rejuvenate the central bank and its monetary policy. The Socialist government of Francois Mitterrand was noted for its early mis-givings over granting some degree of independence to the Banque de France, from its role of being a mere political tool. As late as the early 1980s, in his aborted dash to singularly re-inflate the economy of France, the Banque de France was used to engineer a re-inflation that saw a collapse in the franc and the encouragement of an even higher rate of hyper-inflation, as the country continued to reel from O.P.E.C. oil domination within the industrialised world.

The sudden turn in the Mitterrand government's dash to reinflate its economy, came as a result of fierce discussions and consultations within Europe as well as the G•7. His predecessor, Valérie Giscard-d'Estaing, and Germany's Chancellor Helmut Schmidt, agreed to introduce and create what became known as the Exchange Rate Mechanism (ERM) in a broader European Monetary System (EMS). What they hoped to accomplish by the ERM, was to tie the fluctuation of European exchange rates, so as to remove a further ineffi-ciency in European regional trade, and to deepen integration in Europe.

The ERM project was the predecessor to the single European market, and the single European currency, the "Euro." Mitterrand deviated from this initial strategy, by pursuing an extreme Socialist program that used the Banque de France to attain the Socialist party's direct political goals. This, however, was very short-lived, as other G•7 leaders persuaded him that the ERM strategy developed by his predecessor and Helmut Schmidt of Germany, was the only alternative for Europe.

Both France and Italy moved to tie their exchange rates to the Deutsche mark, hence buying credibility from the strength of the reputation of the Bundesbank. Created after the second world war, the Bundesbank had a direct mandate to ensure price stability in Germany. By the 1950s, it began achieving a success rate that was second to none, not only within Europe, but also relative to the performance of the U.S. Federal Reserve. It can be argued that the Bundesbank was one of the most successful banking institutions in modern history, and definitely the pre-eminent central bank in the latter half of the twentieth century.

The Bundesbank was also one of very few that strictly targeted the growth of broad money supply, or M3, by its technical definition. By contrast, this feat was attempted by the Federal Reserve in 1979, under Paul Volcker, but quickly abandoned in favour of a more eclectic monetary policy rule. By the time Alan Greenspan assumed his duty at the Fed in 1987, strict monetary targeting as an experiment was left for historians to evaluate. The Bundesbank, however, displayed great skill in targeting broad money, hence maintaining control over inflation, even during the chaotic period of spiralling oil prices and O.P.E.C. power in the 1970s. As an oil importer, Germany was subjected to a massive external shock from the price increases, but the Bundesbank was able to skillfully engineer a low rate of inflation within the five to seven percent range during this period. Its skills in central banking became a well-known fact by the mid 1980s, as the political inertia for the single currency was stepped up by European Commission President Jacques Delors.

By tying their currencies to the German mark, the Banque de France, Banca Italia and the Banca Espana, were able to become appendages of the Bundesbank. Just like the Federal Reserve system in the U.S. has regional Fed banks in cities such as Kansas City, Dallas, St. Louis and Atlanta, Europe now had an emerging European central bank; the Bundesbank, and a number of regional quasi-Bundesbanks in France, Italy, Spain and the Benelux countries. No longer could money supply regulation be practiced domestically. It was now completely to be determined in Frankfurt. Consequently, these countries signed away a great deal of their political freedom to the whims of the Bundesbank.

Tensions were running at a high when the Berlin Wall collapsed in 1989, and east Germany was finally re-integrated with west Germany. Running against the advice of then President of the Bundesbank, Karl Otto Pöhl, Helmut Kohl, now known as the "great German unifier" opted to honour east German savings and costs at an absurdly inflated rate of conversion. Instead of giving 0.5 Deutsche marks, for every 1 eastern mark, he over-ruled the Bundesbank and granted equality to each east German mark. He effectively allowed the citizens of east Germany to trade one old communist era mark for one strong Deutsche mark. This had an enormous boom impact on the unified Germany initially, but also led to inflationary pressures with a lag of one to two years. The Bundesbank saw its measure of M3 rise to unacceptable levels, as it moved to wring out inflation by raising its discount and lombard interest rates.
The re-unification of the two Germany's almost derailed the entire movement towards a single European currency, as countries such as Italy and France needed to match the German internal rate increases to stabilise their pegged currencies. After hedge fund financier George Soros, effectively took the pound ster-

ling out of play in 1992, the Italian lira was the next to break out of its peg with the Deutsche mark. The Bundesbank was notable for its single-minded concentration only on managing the surging rate of domestic inflation in the early years of re-unification. It was severely reprimanded and criticised by both Brussels and Paris throughout the early 1990s. The pressure of high interest rates in Germany, which needed to be matched by France, Italy, Spain and the Benelux countries in order to preserve the exchange rate peg through the E.R.M., exacted a severe cost on the regional European economic infrastructure by delivering permanently high rates of unemployment. The pressures became so severe, that the only way by which the E.R.M. could be salvaged was via a unilateral decision by EU members in the summer of 1993, to widen the fluctuation bands of the E.R.M. from 2.25 percent to fifteen percent.

The rigid monetary targeting rule practiced by the Bundesbank left no room for flexibility in a period of immense structural transformation. Had the Bundesbank adopted the constitution of the Federal Reserve, with a loose promise to uphold both growth as well as a low inflation rate, the E.R.M. could still have been preserved in its original form, and George Soros may just have been another eccentric hedge fund manager without gaining the notoriety that he became known for throughout this period of crises.

This episode, which ultimately led up to the creation of the single currency and the faceless European Central Bank, is significant in that it can be interpreted as an experiment embedded in the new system of globalisation and general deflationary environment. Does the new post-Cold War climate really need such discipline in Central banking? Do monetary targets go too far and exacerbate a situation that is already naturally friendly to low rates of inflation? What the Bundesbank has accomplished was admirable throughout the Cold War era, especially during the O.P.E.C. oil price shocks of the 1970s. Its achievement of delivering inflation rates within the five to seven percent target has contributed positively to the history of money and banking.

The forerunner of the Bundesbank, the European Central Bank (E.C.B.) under former Governor of the Nederlandsche Bank, Wim Duisenberg, has a constitution that is different from the Bundesbank. Gone are the strict monetary targets in favour of an eclectic policy rule favouring a combination of business activity, inflation or deflation and regional disparities. Policy has now been dispersed over the entire European region, with Germany and France still the dominant economic engines, but with an eye also towards Spain, Italy and Portugal. The E.C.B. is more in tune with the new post-Cold War climate under the new system of globalisation, and is looking more and more similar to the Federal Reserve. Ironically, the concern over inflation in the early German unification period of the 1990s, has been transformed into one of deflation and regional disparities within Europe in the latter half of the decade.

Under a period of deflation or stable pricing, central bankers such as Alan Greenspan have been struggling to understand the emerging role of their institutions under the new system of globalisation. Record levels of employment in the U.S. and yet no real signs of inflationary pressure, together with productivity growth far in excess of the natural long term trend of just over two percent, has created a policy vacuum at the Fed.

The recent move to raise rates once again in the spring of 2000, followed the spreading fears from the global financial meltdown in 1997, after the Asian financial crisis spread to the Russian default, hammering all emerging market investors in the process. The aggressive move to add liquidity into the global financial system by the Fed, acted to neutralise further financial panic in global markets. The last vestiges of the crises was the devaluation of the Brazilian Real, after which the Fed adopted a more domestic policy bias, leading to five recent, and in my opinion, completely baseless and unwarranted rate increases.

After its admirable monetary management of the global crises in east Asia and the emerging economies, the Fed has fallen into a Cold War mode of thinking. Yes, unemployment in the U.S. is at a record low level, and growth is way above the historical trend, but inflation just does not factor into the new climate. High technology and the growing use of the internet will ensure that electronic commerce plays its role in holding down price increases. Competition at the consumer retail level is higher than it has ever been, and since over two-thirds of the U.S. economy is driven by consumption spending, the wide array of new products and imported products that are being made available are a natural hedge against price increases. The Fed must realise that its stand in favour of higher interest rates, and higher real interest rates for that matter, will adversely impact the old economy much more than it will the high technology sector, further causing a rift between the performance of these two broad sectoral groupings. The Fed is recently behaving as though it does not know where to turn, it is directionless and is under the illusion that inflation is once again a major threat to stable money, when in fact deflation is the greater problem, elevated even further by the growth in real short term interest rates.

THE FREE TRADE ERA

Global free trade did not exist in the Cold War era, but was the pre-dominant system of the late nineteenth century. The common characteristic of capital flows during this period was the gold standard, where a country with a trade deficit, exported physical gold bullion thereby naturally reducing its domestic money supply, which was ultimately backed by the gold standard. In this respect, an equilibrium in the international trading system was always synchronised with the monetary conditions domestically. A country in deficit on its trade accounts, would experience an outflow of bullion, reducing its domestic money supply, hence bringing its own product prices down so that it would become globally competitive once again, and ultimately experience a balance of payments surplus; re-attracting gold bullion and leading to an inflationary expansion of its money supply domestically once again. This was the free trade system that functioned prior to the advent of the Cold War.

During the latter stages of the Cold War, and as early as the move by Giscard d'Estaing and Helmut Schmidt to propose a fixing of European exchange rates in the Exchange Rate Mechanism by 1979, the G•7 economy of advanced industrialised countries began to experience a natural resurgence in international trade. The proximity of European countries within one region the size of the Province of Ontario, made trade an undeniable fact of European economic life. The motivation for creating a European single currency was ingrained in many different facets of European life, but the deepening of the single common market was front and foremost. Trade, exchange rates and monetary policy were intimately linked within the region, and any move to enhance trade was vital to creating the foundations for dynamic growth in business activity.

What began as a project to deepen the European common market, together with the European political process, so as to avoid any resurgence of hostilities and a possible third world war, began to spread to North America. The idea of free trade was already very much a feature of U.S. and Canadian commercial relations. The sheer size of the U.S. market, was always a major factor in deciding to locate production facilities in Canada by European corporations. More than one-third of Canadian business is based on orders originating in the U.S., and the entire currency politics surrounding the Canadian dollar are all based on this trading relationship.

Ironically, trade, communications and finance are all intimately tied together. Without having international trade, international capital flows would not come about. Without the information revolution, trade opportunities would not be known. And without risk capital devoted to trade finance, trade flows would be difficult to facilitate. During the Cold War system, trade was a tool of foreign policy. Only within the G•7 countries could trade move efficiently along, but any relations with what were then termed as "developing" countries (present day equivalent to emerging markets), were scrutinised for what types of allegiance they exhibited towards free market ideology when invoking the U.S. perspective. Likewise, the Soviet Union bribed all of its proxy countries with very generous development aid, built inefficient factories and supplied the necessities of life, including inferior Lada cars, in order to gain the allegiance of their proxies in solidarity with the Communist ideology. During the Cold War, trade was very much tied in with foreign policy and the competition between free market ideology and communism. In that respect, it was also tied to aid proxies such as Fidel Castro in Cuba and Saddam Hussein in Iraq. In a similar fashion, the U.S. tied its trade policy with generous financial and industrial support to its ideological allies in western Europe, Israel and Egypt.

As globalisation planted its early seeds in the 1980s, it both contributed and was a part of the process of opening up markets to freer trade relations. In North America, Canadian Prime Minister Brian Mulroney aggressively moved to validate what was long a feature of Canadian economic life, by negotiating the controversial Free Trade Agreement (FTA) with the U.S. Mulroney's government became one of the most vilified governments in Canadian history, as public opinion was of the view that the FTA contributed to one of its deepest and most prolonged depressions in history in the early 1990s. The deflation that hit the Canadian economy during this period lost an entire generation. However, the symptoms were more the direct result of the collapse of the Berlin Wall, than they were from the perceived "sell-out" from the Free Trade Agreement with the U.S.

In essence, the Free Trade Agreement was really a document that had US-Canadian automotive trade in mind. Back in the 1960s, some very cunning Canadian civil servants negotiated what became one of the best bilateral treaties in the world. The Auto Pact stipulated that for each class of vehicle sold in Canada, a vehicle of equal value in the same class had to be produced, thereby circumventing any permanent balance of trade deficit that would have inevitably have been the result with the U.S., and a permanent drag on the Canadian dollar. The Free Trade Agreement retained the main features of the Auto Pact, thereby gaining the support of the trade union (CAW), but laid a framework for further liberalisation when Mexico became a member under the newly-expanded North American Free Trade Agreement, or Nafta for short.

Despite this, from the vantage point of the North American automotive industry, the FTA had nothing to do with Nafta from a legal and technical angle. A further difference, was that the FTA was far more auto issues-driven than Nafta, but that the original Auto Pact was far easier to administer at the borders. Moreover, the penalty for not meeting the one-to-one sales to production ratio in Canada was removed from Nafta, mainly due to the superior negotiating skills of the U.S. trade representatives, effectively eliminating the old Auto Pact effects.

By the time automotive trade became more liberalised, Canadian assembly operations had already attained a high level of efficiency, as had the entire auto industry by moving more and more towards automation and robotics. The auto industry was on the leading edge of technology, and the Auto Pact became less of a concern to Canadian negotiators. What was once an industry where the working classes could earn a decent standard of living by working at menial tasks on an assembly line, was anything but in the era of growing globalisation. The Canadian Auto Workers (CAW) union was powerful, but it was aging and dwindling in numbers. The "Big 3" auto manufacturers; Ford, DaimlerChrysler and General Motors, moved to create a global supply-chain for the assembly of their vehicles. Steering wheels would be produced in Belgium, engines would be produced in Detroit and chassis may be produced in Brazil or in Mexico. Included within this supply chain were the very efficient Canadian assembly plants in Oakville, Oshawa and Windsor. No longer, in this new era of globalisation, were instruments such as the Auto Pact necessary or vital to the survival of a Canadian assembly industry. Canadian automotive production came of age as globalisation took off.

Trade, as a component of economic growth has become more prominent in the post-Cold War world. Many countries within the G•7 relied entirely on exports during the early 1990s, to ensure that their depressed local economies could be hedged by business generated in faster-growing emerging markets. Free Trade and globalisation have created opportunities for G•7 based companies everywhere to the point that in many cases, exports count for a greater proportion of overall business, than do orders generated in their respective domestic economies. There is stiff competition in Asian emerging markets among all of the members of the G•7. In Canada, the government's initiatives on trade are well publicised and promoted to the media. These "Team Canada" trade missions to Asia, Latin America, Europe and the Middle East are a partnership between the foreign service and private companies.

The Canadian economy was hit hard as the new system came into effect, and exports were promoted very hard in order to offset the decline in government subsidies and deficit spending. Likewise, the effects of globalisation and the high rates of interest in Europe, adversely affected France. Had it not been for exports, the French economy would have hit levels of unemployment that could have triggered a revolution.

Trade was also an area in which the newly emerging market countries of Europe and Asia could ease their transition to a free market system. Unfortunately, the G•7 group was less than willing to open up to these new economies in order to facilitate their development. This is most evident in the on-going discussions between the European Union in Brussels, and those wishing to become full members of the economic union, such as Poland, Hungary and the Czech Republic. All of these countries are very close to the standard of living available within the EU, but the EU is less than determined to promote the fast-tracking of this group. With the exception of Germany, many EU countries in the Mediterranean and the south look at the newly emerged countries as both a threat to their EU development grants, as well as the more competitive climate that their exports would create within the EU. Administrative reforms in the voting procedures in Brussels have not advanced to a level where a new group of three to four central European countries could be accommodated. These countries find themselves in an awkward position, after ten years from the collapse of the Berlin Wall, the initial promises of embracing them in the heart of Europe, have been very long in coming. Unfortunately, this blockage of membership in the EU, has made the economic life in central Europe come up short to its true potential. The only way to ensure that the free market system optimally affects the emerging market countries, is by wholly and effectively tying them into the markets of the G•7 and the European Union.

Compared to the previous era of globalisation in the late nineteenth century, the trade balance has come to assume a far less important role in determining currency values in relation to the past decade. Currently, trade flows fall well below in importance, relative to the effects that investment capital has had on currency values and central banking practices. Both international portfolio investment, as well as cross border mergers and acquisitions overshadow the money flows that are attributed to international trade. Based on this evidence, financial innovation, together with global communications will both act to push international trade down even further over the next five years. Whether or not trade can increase its share of the overall world income produced is not certain, except that the recent developments in finance will become constant influences in the promotion of business relations outside of national borders.

SOROS AND THE "BIG PICTURE"

On the rare occasion, the "boring" financial industry tends to produce celebrities of its own. During the 1970s, it was Felix Rohatyn, the former Partner of Wall Street investment bank, Lazard Brothers, that was credited in saving New York City from inevitable bankruptcy. The 1980s was synonymous with the notorious Wall Street corporate raiders, Michael Milken and Ivan Boesky, while the collapse of the pound sterling in 1992, netted hedge fund operator George Soros a massive fortune. To this day, the patriotic English still grumble at the mention of Soros' name. What George Soros has accomplished by breaking the fixing of Sterling in the Exchange Rate Mechanism, was to signal to the world that the new era of free capital mobility, coupled with the ease in communication, has the ability to cripple governments and eminent institutions in a matter of minutes, or even seconds.

The growing global capital pool and the speed in which it can be invested in various countries, and then re-patriated, has produced a system that can be lethal to those that are elected to formulate policy. Any government that desires a higher standard of living, cannot escape foreign portfolio investment any longer. Not only are foreign investors calling the shots, but also, investors that are based locally now have the option to send their money abroad, even though their countries are officially closed, or have some vestiges remaining that control foreign exchange. What this means to policy makers, is that a new level of efficiency has been placed on their shoulders. With this highly efficient system that sends money spinning around the world, comes the obligations to restructure the local banking system and stock market so that transparency is never in doubt. The catch-phrase in the 1990s, has been that if investors perceive a country to be open and transparent, such that money can flow in and out at the click of a mouse, then the country in question will be the ultimate beneficiary over the longer term. Just look at Hong Kong, the U.K. and the U.S.

George Soros made a fortune in hedging situations that were inconsistent with the general trend towards open and efficient markets. Anytime when evidence existed of a fundamental overshoot in one market, he would leverage his bet that it would eventually come back to its fundamental values. For instance, the pound sterling initially joined the E.R.M. at an overly inflated price, in relation to the Deutsche mark and the general basket of European currencies. The hard landing in the U.K. in the early part of the 1990s, was no different from that in most of the Anglo-saxon countries, including the U.S. The collapse of the commercial real-estate market in the U.K., symbolised by the problems at Canary Wharf, wiped out most private developers in London. It sent the local, intensely real estate-oriented economy into a deep recession, meanwhile, rates were based on the over-inflated conditions in Germany shortly after re-unification.

George Soros made a common-sense bet that sterling could not continue at such an inflated level, with inflated interest rates serving to keep it artificially propped-up in the E.R.M. With the help of the London market's liquidity, he was able to effectively sell it short, by selling the sterling that he did not hold in the hopes of buying it back at a later date at a far cheaper price. This scenario materialised, sterling was dropped from the E.R.M., and the former Minister of the Exchequer, Norman Lamont, was made the scape-goat in British politics and had to tender a reluctant resignation to the Prime Minister at the time, John Major. Soros' bet paid off handsomely; created a historical event in the process and elevated him to celebrity status, which he uses to great effect even today.

It is interesting to note, however, that this same George Soros, has gone on record in communicating to his investors that returns of the type made during the sterling debacle, are much harder to make as globalisation advances further. In essence, Soros is a "fundamental" investor, or one that arbitrages situations that are not rational or consistent with free market ideology. In the case of sterling, it was not consistent with its natural free market level, since the E.R.M. propped it up artificially, creating great misery and financial distress in the British economy in the early part of the decade.

As the 1990s progressed, and the internet added even more transparency to financial markets, it overshot its point where financial valuations were true reflections of real economic activity. In other words, does the stock market make sense where it currently rests? What can we make of the wild valuations in the price/earnings ratios of newly formed internet companies? Does Soros have it right, when he says that he can no longer expect to make returns in excess of thirty percent for his funds, when the current gyrations in the markets are very difficult to value on a sensible or fundamental basis? Capital markets and the global flows of money have become overly transparent in many ways. In fact, the culture of investment has spread so rapidly, that traders are no longer buying and selling based on fundamental values, but are doing so based on the movement of the stock or currency in itself. In this respect, the movement of financial assets has become a "casino." Soros knows and understands this, as does U.S. investor Warren Buffet, who openly admits his shortcomings in understanding the new high tech economy.

The click of the mouse has made it possible to shuffle the deck globally. There are no more barriers in buying stocks anywhere in the world, and as stock markets form "electronic" alliances, the prospect of twenty-four hour trading is at hand. Under such a system, the creation of a huge electronic herd of investors will wreak havoc on governments everywhere, which are deemed as being untrustworthy or not open to the concept of quick entry and exit of capital. The challenges that will come about under such a fast-paced system of investing, will ensure that more and more regions of the world that were perceived as once being "closed," will be connected and making a pitch to powerful pension fund managers in hoping to attract their share of this growing pool of global money.

George Soros is right in that fundamentals don't mean too much any more when it comes to the valuation of currencies or stocks. What is most important now, in order to arbitrage gains in the markets, is the investors' or money managers' nerve in timing the trend in this new casino economy. The fund managers job has become harder as the decade has progressed. So much so that venture capital investing in risky biotechnology ventures has now become commonplace, and will only continue to expand as more and more money will be added to this internationally mobile pool of capital. In essence, it seems that the time to have benefited from playing the fundamentals game passed when George Soros hammered sterling out of the E.R.M. Shortly thereafter, opportunities for hedge funds to score big became less and less apparent as the 1990s progressed. The time to have gotten in and played the "fundamentalist" game in investing seems to have been long gone, as more emerging market countries adopt a common managerial standard and move ever more closer to the standard of transparency evident among the G•7.

SHOULD I BUY FORD OR U.S. TREASURIES?

Big multinational companies are in direct competition with governments when it comes to attracting investment capital. Globalisation has resulted in the polarisation of the corporate sector, as big companies that were run inefficiently in the 1980s have gone on a merger and acquisition binge in the nineties. What was supposed to have been a period that encouraged more competition in all markets, has resulted in big companies consolidating their positions in market share domestically, and then trying to extend these shares globally. The internet economy and escalating pricing competition that it is supposed to bring, has created a defensive climate among some of the most well known name brands in the world. This development was not expected, and was not supposed to catch the Fortune 1000 off-guard as it has. The consolation to consumers has in fact been the price competition that the internet economy is promising, in order to offset the large mergers that have become a hallmark of the latter years in the 1990s.

Although the Cold War years were notable for inefficiencies and guaranteed local market shares for many of the largest brands, there were early developments in financial engineering, which drove many companies to restructure their balance sheets so as to raise shareholder values. The late 1980s were notable for leveraged buy-outs, which served to increase shareholder value and buy-back the excess supply of stock that was floated throughout the 1970s. During this period of inflation and rising oil prices, the stock market was at one of its worst performance levels in history, as firms predominantly financed each other via share issues, holding very little debt on their balance sheets. In a way, it was ironical, that a period of low corporate debt was associated with such a disappointing performance in their share prices. What this meant, however, is that there was an optimal debt to equity ratio that companies should strive for in order to maximise their share prices. This is what essentially turned their fortunes around in the 1980s.

The move to raise share performance co-incided with many developments that were new. For one, senior executives drew a compensation package that included not only a negotiated wage, but also stock options which often far exceeded the wage on offer. There was the creation of direct incentives linking the performance of the company on a quarterly basis, to the eventual compensation paid to management. Furthermore, companies saw the opportunity to become lean and mean through the introduction of information technology. No longer was it necessary to carry the "inverted pyramid" structure which became such a symbol of corporate life throughout the 1960s and the 1970s. For example, in the fast-changing world of banking, a Credit Division which at one time relied on the analysis of a staff of five people, could now make do with two. The structure was essentially "flattened" by the adoption of information technology, computers and the internet.

The efficient structure that was forced upon the corporate sector, as shareholder value became the predominant religion, brought continuous capital gains to the largest and most well-run companies. Notable were General Electric, IBM, Ford and Intel that immediately come to mind, but the overall general direction of this trend was unmistakable. Instead of causing lower share prices, the post-Cold War period of disinflation only raised the real value of these "blue-chip" stocks. Pension fund managers looked at these developments with great interest in the early 1990s, as the "military-industrial complex" driven economy of the 1980s, was replaced by the competitiveness-seeking; shareholder value driven economy of the 1990s. Disinflation and outright deflation, did not destroy share values, as these companies were able to extract enough value from cost savings, yet maintain a spectacular growth rate in their profits to warrant investor interest. They were also able to maintain their domestic market shares via mergers or acquisitions, and expand globally via this strategy in order to solidify the upward progress of their share prices.

The question facing many portfolio investment managers, as well as private investors and savers, concerned the performance of relatively risk-free government debt instruments. U.S. Treasury bonds and commercial bank savings deposits were under increasing scrutiny in terms of the returns that were on offer. Institutional investors increasingly looked to raise their holdings of blue-chip stocks at the expense of bond holdings. The issue was presented as: Should I buy Ford or should I keep my money in U.S. Treasury bills? If the governments moved to expand their budgets by raising spending, they would be in direct competition with Ford, IBM and General Electric more now, than ever before in history. By doing so, would have created increasingly divergent real rates of interest, adding further stress to the overall climate of greater competition and disinflation throughout the 1990s.

In this sense, the preference between holding government investment paper and stocks, became directly competitive with one another. Fortunately, the era of surplus budgets did not require more borrowings, hence creating a treasury bond and bill buy-back program that was instituted by Treasury Secretary Lawrence Summers. The buy-back of treasuries co-incided with greater revenues from financial transaction turnover in the booming stock markets. It was now easier to levy taxes on capital gains and paper turnover and trading profits, than it was on the old economy firms producing some type of goods. The collection of tax revenues was far more simpler when levied on financial instruments turnover, which is precisely what happened in the latter half of the Clinton Administration's mandate.

This had the overall effect of reducing the supply of government bonds in the U.S., down to where the lower level of demand existed for these assets. In effect, the well-performing blue-chip equities became a proxy for conservative savers, who usually preferred to maintain savings and term deposits in either the New York money centre banks or large regionals. This process seemed all too natural, as the rise of the equity culture driven by returns over the recent past added to the coffers of the Treasury, thereby automatically reducing the need for more bond issues to finance the inner workings of the government. The rise of stocks and the fall of bonds seemed to be a science in itself, and enabled the effective reduction of long term interest rates.

Once again, the U.S. was the leader in this financing trend within the G•7, as the UK, Canada and even France, all began to experience the exact same phenomenon. Notable among these countries was the developments of a solid equity culture in both France and in Germany, and for the first time ever, the budget of the European Union in Brussels moved to a position of surplus!

European stock markets experienced something that they never did before. They generated an enormous level of interest in their prized "blue-chip" equities, under a fast developing acceptance by the public in holding their savings through these vehicles. For the first time, the DAX in Frankfurt and the CAC-40 index in Paris began to break away from the rigid link that they always had with the developments on the Dow Jones Industrial Averages. There was a great deal of evidence that the U.S. markets always laid the framework for the general direction of stocks around the world. During the 1990s, this relationship became more looser, as the structural shift that began in the U.S., favouring stocks over bond investments, became well ingrained in Europe taking on an inertia of its own which was specific to the European region.

The case of Italy is most striking, as the culture of bond investing was always well established during the Cold War era. Italian savers were always inclined to buy local government, lira-denominated bonds, thereby fueling the surging deficits that became a common feature during the 1970s and the 1980s in Italy. The habits of the investing public were welcomed by the political classes, as they became addicted to this behaviour of savers supplying a constant and ready supply of savings in order to finance the growing deficits during this time. It was only recently, when Italy was forced to invoke measures of austerity in the run-up to joining the European single currency, that its reliance on deficit finance was upset in the process. The Maastricht Treaty which created the framework for participation in the single currency, stipulated that the debt to GDP of each country could not exceed sixty percent. Italy was as high as 140 percent, all of which created a huge stock of bonds that were readily snapped up by Italian savers; in turn feeding the vicious debt spiral in the whole process.

During the Cold War, Italian stock market investing was more or less limited to a handful of patriarch-controlled stocks. Family-controlled industrial groupings such as Fiat and Olivetti were basically all that was available to those interested in the Milan stock markets. These privately-controlled groups were also heavily regulated by the political process in Italy, and were not operated under the axioms of maximising profits or shareholder value. Politicians usually dictated terms and parameters to these companies, and a great deal of attention was paid to their employment practices and their inclination towards promoting regional industrial development within Italy. Moreover, their CEOs could be far more accurately described as "leaders" in the spirit of sharing or dividing powers with the political class. People such as Gianni Agnelli of Fiat and Carlo De Benedetti of Olivetti, were prolific and a major force within Italian political-economic relations. In essence, their roles were far greater than just being CEOs.

Slowly, the culture began to change, as early signs of equity market development sprang to life when Olivetti under Carlo De Benedetti launched an uncharacteristically hostile bid for Belgian political-industrial conglomerate, Société Générale in 1986. This was unique, in that it foreshadowed a change in investor relations in Europe, and although unsuccessful, it began to inject a different set of rules in the game. In a way, De Benedetti's move against Société Générale proved to be very much at the cutting-edge in the hostile takeovers that ensued in the U.S. a year or two later. In that respect, De Benedetti was ahead of the pack, even ahead of the traditional trend-setting financiers in the U.S.

As the Cold War ended, the Italian political system went on trial. Many of the most prolific political power brokers, such as Giulio Andreotti and Bettino Craxi, either went on trial, or were sent into self-imposed exile. Craxi's self-imposed exile in Tunisia ended in his death of natural causes, even though his return to Italy would have been met with an immediate trial over allegations of corruption when he was the Socialist Prime Minister in the 1980s. The financial effect of all of this was a natural call for less government, as a new political party was formed under Umberto Bossi, called the Northern separatist League, or "Liga" for short. Bossi's mandate was to break away from the free-spending south, using the mafia association and corruption trials of Andreotti and Craxi, as a rallying cry for a smaller budget and the ultimate independence of the prosperous northern regions.

In this respect, the domestic political scene embraced and was conducive to less government in Italy in the 1990s. This internal calling was consistent with the external handcuffs being placed on Italian politicians by the Maastricht Treaty and plans to make Italy a founding member of the single currency. What ensued was radical restructuring of stock market listed companies, consistent with the overall trend towards adopting high technology and intense managerial efficiency in all of the G•7 countries.

As the 1990s progressed, so did Italy's equity culture to a point where it is the highest per capita user of mobile telephone technology in Europe. Likewise, acceptance of the internet has been spectacular so far, as many IPOs throughout Europe have certainly been inclusive towards Italian companies. The defining characteristic of the fast developing equity culture, is the decline in interest in channeling savings into the traditionally popular domestic bond markets. For the first time, evidence has surfaced of armies of Italian day-traders, which are bound to match and even surpass the phenomenon that is currently evident throughout the U.S. All of these advances and the natural retreat of the bond as the traditional outlet to Italian savers, brilliantly defines the overall trend within the G•7 that is favouring "blue-chip" stocks as the ultimate post-Cold War savings vehicle.

MILLIONS OF FUNDS AND
ONE GLOBAL STOCK MARKET

During the Cold War, investment funds, mutual funds and pension funds were a
relatively unknown quantity, while global or international funds were almost
non-existent except for the rare few managed by private banks in off-shore centres. It was only very recently in the late 1980s, that European countries joining
the single currency program, moved to liberalise capital flows within the
region. More significantly, were the proliferation of funds in the U.S. and in
Canada throughout the 1990s, since Europeans were already accustomed to
having off-shore countries that were within easy reach of an afternoon's drive.
Luxembourg, Switzerland, Monaco, Andorra, Trieste and even Austria could
all be characterised as appealing to most heavily-taxed European citizens.
These off-shore centres were always able to appeal to the citizens of major G•7
European countries. In effect, the region of Ticino and Lugano were the preserve of Milan's businesspeople, while Luxembourg was the preserve of the
tax-averse Belgians and Alsace Germans. Countries such as Luxembourg are
presently in the forefront of debate within the European Union, as banking
laws within the single currency zone mobilise to become uniform. To now,
Switzerland has opted to be excluded from any moves to become absorbed
within the single currency program in order to preserve its banking tradition.

Aside from the influence of the multi-faceted off-shore centres in the Euro
zone, the Cold War years were more defined by regionalism within Europe.
Each region was closed to most of its savers and investors, and those that were
the clients of the off-shore network, could be better described as being within a
minority. Stock markets were exclusively national in spirit, with almost no
cross-listings of equities. Efficiency was compromised throughout this period,
with the Chairman of the Vienna Stock Exchange even going as far as openly
admitting that his Exchange was mainly there for reasons of folklore, and an
addition to the overall Austrian heritage and culture. Trading volumes were so
small and insignificant, that the institution was far from being a regional profit
centre in finance and banking.

The closure of many regions politically, as well as financially via a multitude
of customs duties, stamp duties and capital controls, prevented a deepening of
financial markets throughout this period in European countries. The predomi-
nance of banking credits available to finance enterprises in most countries and
an underdeveloped equity culture prevented the growth in investment funds,
not to mention the effects of capital controls. Since most Central Banks had not
yet gained their independence from their respective Ministers of Finance, monetary relations still were governed by the overhang created in international cap-

ital markets when the Bretton-Woods system broke down in 1972, during the Nixon Administration and the implementation of wage and price controls. The fixing of exchange rates that Bretton-Woods was created to guide and administer, placed rigid constraints on the flow of capital since markets had not yet "deepened" adequately, and trade still made up a major component of international capital flows throughout the 1970s, playing off surplus countries with deficit countries. The mentality created by this "trade-balancing" politics from the Bretton-Woods era exacted an enormous effect on moves towards liberalising international capital flows. Just the thought of fixing exchange rates for such a very long period of time after the second world war, together with trade balancing politics was enough to derail any moves to liberalise capital flows. Opening up the capital account of countries was not something that politicians were so quickly prepared to experiment with. After all, trade relations still governed international goods, as well as financial flows.

During the Cold War, there were many stock exchanges and few private investment funds. Technology was still analog, and the political command economy created the rules of engagement for both west and east. Further, pensions were centrally planned, administered and mainly collected by the "pay-as-you-go" system, where younger generations financed the benefits of the elderly. Very few countries had an equity culture, since stock markets were considered as being too risky with no promise of stability to savers.

Although foreign direct investment flows were a permanent feature throughout the Cold War, the companies deciding to build a plant on a greenfield site still financed such ventures from their domestic pool of capital. Very rarely did Ford or Daimler Benz opt to raise capital for their projects in their host countries, let alone to cross-list their shares in either the U.S. or in Frankfurt. The latter became a symbol of the opening of capital flows and only until full liberalisation had occurred in the 1990s, were cross listings of shares of major corporations visible on a number of major stock markets.

The single European currency project, with the driving political will of Helmut Kohl of Germany and Francois Mitterrand of France, was also a guiding influence for the liberalisation of capital flows. Full liberalisation was slowly phased in over time, and if there was a single positive development that came out of the entire single currency project, it was the push towards full capital liberalisation in areas of Europe, that just ten years ago, were vehemently opposed to any such moves. In the initial years of capital liberalisation, national stock exchanges benefited from the increasing volumes of trading from various countries within the European Union. Only until the mid 1990s, did the advent of the internet and day trading send a wake up call to each national exchange, that in some cases, was an acknowledgment towards the eventual consolidation within Europe and beyond. Former General Secretary of the

European Federation of Stock Exchanges, Jean-Pierre Paelinck, told me in our interview that he could not conceive of the day when a national presence in listing shares within Europe was no longer an administrative necessity. However, as the 1990s drew to a close, the national stock market apparatus was poised for extinction. Recently, the London Stock Exchange and the Deutsche Börse, have announced a very difficult, yet necessary merger. Contra to this announcement, was the move to merge the Paris, Amsterdam and the diminutive Brussels Exchange in a bloc that for the time being is in response to the London-Frankfurt axis created. What seems as two competing blocs for trading volumes, will over the next several years become a merged entity yet again. The pace of technological change will outpace the special national interest groups that have always governed these stock exchanges in the past, and who have always maintained a sense of regional autonomy in Europe, and moreover, have managed to keep financial systems separate and monopolistically controlled all in the name of national regulatory interest.

The proliferation of investment funds has coincided with the re-engineering of corporate balance sheets in the 1980s. Equity funds have exploded in tandem with the optimal float that companies have engineered over the latter half of the 1980s. The situation went from too much equity and not enough debt in the 1970s, to an episode in the 1980s, where leveraged buy-outs and share buy-backs breathed some life back into stock returns. Also, executive incentive schemes such as share options based on meeting profitability targets became commonplace. Before equity funds could explode by the thousands, there had to be a re-engineering of balance sheets, and the optimal float of supply outstanding for any movement upward in values. As the 1990s progressed, so did stock gains, which created more interest among savers holding interest-bearing investments, which in turn launched a multitude of mutual funds in every corner of the world. In short, the financial infrastructure during the transition went from many national stock exchanges and just a handful of investment funds, to "one global stock exchange and a million investment funds."

MERGERS AND ACQUISITIONS

One thing notable in the more serious daily news media, is the proliferation of headline stories that centred around the growing trend towards mergers and acquisitions. It seems that nuclear bombs and weapons of mutually assured destruction have been replaced by news of AOL buying out Time Warner, or mobile phone group Vodafone of the UK, buying out Mannesmann of Germany or even French auto group Renault taking over the near-bankrupt Nissan Motor of Japan. Never before have companies called on their foreign competitors to join together in defending market share, as they have in the decade of the 1990s that became increasingly defined by this new system called "globalisation." Instead of embracing the greater competition domestically and internationally, the 1990s was a transition period that was defined by defensive actions by the largest "blue-chip" multinationals to limit competition against their market shares and interests. It was also a decade of heightened competition that was driven by technological changes, and restricted only to the high tech infrastructure producing sector at the outset. The more mature industries and brand names, first moved defensively to merge and acquire, so as to defend their existing market shares, but afterwards the push was on to aggressively use the new technologies of the internet and communications to expand their market shares organically.

The best example of troubled sectors under this rapidly changing period of technological changes, were in the food processing and consumer products industries. Analysts and investors came down hard on companies such as Procter and Gamble, Nabisco and Heinz, as evidence of static market share became more and more apparent as the decade moved along. In one day, Procter and Gamble's share price dropped by almost fifty percent, as word spread that the company did not achieve analysts' earnings expectations. Investors were left perplexed as to how the new internet e-commerce solutions could be successfully implemented in such a traditional sector. It was believed that avenues of growth in this sector were already exhausted by the wholesale and retail distribution systems, and after all, how would households take to ordering groceries online?

The aggressive move to protect global market shares, has made sectors more powerful than nation-states in terms of the resources and income generating activities that they now are able to command. Many investment banks such as Merrill Lynch switched their mode of analysis on a sectoral basis, as opposed to a country-by-country basis. Such a decision by one of the most influential banking institutions globally, says plenty about the changing balance of power between large companies that are getting even larger, and the governments of nation-states, that have been shrinking and losing power. Many political leaders, instead of shaping activist policies of the kind evident in the 1970s, are now forging a consensus that will complement the growing strength of multinational companies, or compete right along with them in terms of attracting financing from investors that have turned their backs on government bond issues, and who are now convinced that the right investment lies in a Merrill Lynch or an IBM. To reclassify bonds in such a way, is to directly pit the management abilities of governments with the managements of the corporate sector. The investor today may ask: "Which investment vehicle today gives me better management prospects for growth in the future. Is it governments via bonds, or is it IBM and Merrill Lynch through their common stocks?" Under those terms, cross border mergers and acquisitions can only continue their run upwards and onwards. The rules of the game have been so radically restructured, that bonds and equities are in direct competition with one another. The corporate sector must do all that it can in the era of 24 hour stock markets, to effectively keep earnings growing. As most large groups wring all of the inefficiencies that they could through the introduction of technology, the natural limits of "flattening" their corporate structures can only be replaced via the growth that is offered through mergers and acquisitions on a global scale.

What has become of anti-trust enforcement throughout this period? Certainly, throughout the 1980s, the Reagan Administration in the US decided to turn a blind eye to industrial combinations that began during the Cold War system. The lower level of activism on behalf of the justice Department's Federal Trade Commission (FTC), carried on into the Bush administration which was in power throughout the formal transformation in the two systems of the Cold War and globalisation, and which was noted for a "do nothing" approach on business issues. After the election of the Clinton Administration, the campaign promise to place markets far and above in importance in the formulation of their fiscal policy and objectives, became almost a natural deterrence to intervention in the growing markets for mergers and acquisitions. This, coupled with the appointment of several notable Wall Street leaders, such as Robert Rubin at the Treasury Department, ensured that the Reagan-Bush era of non-intervention was extended well into this new era.

It can be argued, that the early non-interventionism of the Clinton Administration set the inertia for the entire 1990s, with little scope for reversal once the trend became fully ingrained. In a way, it can be said that the government did not realise that mergers and acquisitions would create a new corporate power structure that would compete head on with the government's themselves, in terms of attracting the appropriate level of capital to maintain their operation an on-going concern. It is no coincidence, when in 1996, the Republican Congress refused to extend the general borrowing powers of the government, that there was barely a panic in the air over the thought that there may be no government apparatus in place for an extended period of time in the U.S. Moreover, this frame of thought can be extended intuitively. As blue-chip stocks come to predominate the investment industry, government financing instruments such as Treasury bills, Bunds, Gilts and Bonds of all shapes and colour fall in importance. Logically, big pension fund portfolios that hold an average of sixty percent of all money in a handful of the most powerful blue-chip companies in the world, leaves a minority of some fourty percent of all financial investments in bonds for governments to finance the on-going needs of the government apparatus. This is a radical switch from the seventy percent of financial investments that were allocated for bonds throughout the 1970s and the 1980s at the height of the Cold War. Globalisation has shifted the balance of power from governments and nation-states, to powerful corporate name brands that transact their business around the world.

The success rate of merging two large companies is less than fifty percent. The more complex the merger, the greater the failure rate. Three very surprising international deals went through very recently. In 1999, pre-eminent French automotive group Renault moved to acquire a controlling stake in Nissan Motor of Japan. Nissan has been in a mess for over a decade, as it was able to post just a few years of profitable performance during this time, with a very weak product line and a management that lacked real vision during a time when competition was heating up. The merger to now is reportedly going as well as it could. The appointment of Carlos Ghosn as the leading "cost-cutter" in Japan, has been met with surprisingly little opposition to now. There have been massive union sponsored protests in Japan over the closure of several assembly plants, but for now the plan to bring Nissan back to profitability seems to be on track.

The enormous problems in the Renault-Nissan deal have to do with managing two distinct cultures within one organisation, who's goal it is to make a profit. Renault has a very strong management on a regional scale, with an impressive product line able to compete within the countries of Europe. Nissan's acquisition was a very bold and opportunistic move, but many experts in the automotive industry such as Toronto based Dennis DesRosiers, feel that the combination will ultimately unravel. His view goes further in putting forward the idea that both Renault and Nissan will be absorbed by the even more powerful DaimlerChrysler. To now, auto sales have been running at record levels, but come a downturn in the industry, and Renault will severely pay for its bold move!

The merger between UK based mobile telephone group Vodafone AirTouch and Mannesmann of Germany is revolutionary. Mannesmann has been a traditional German conglomerate style of company, whose management took pride in its ability to manage a diverse portfolio of industrial interests. For that matter, Mannesmann was known for its moves into mobile telephony, as much as it was known for its traditional presence in the engineering industry in Germany. In many respects, it was a traditional German company. The move by Vodafone AirTouch to buy out Mannesmann, was extraordinary, in that nothing like this was ever known to happen to a German conglomerate champion company. Mergers and acquisitions in Germany never happened, since banks usually held a large cross-shareholding in strategic groups, supplemented by direct government ownership of the shares of important groups. Most German national champions such as Volkswagen and the banks, have as their largest shareholders their respective regional governments. Also, the culture of relying on bank credits did not encourage the development of a formal stock market sector, that would have drawn hostile bids for companies with underperforming managements. In addition, managers were not obliged to maximise profits, hence stock prices were more or less fixed for long periods of time, since corporate production in Germany was organised on a "stakeholder" basis. In this respect, the Supervisory Boards of these companies had labour participation as well as political representatives, and most decisions that were made balanced off the competing interests of each of these factions.

To many, this has become a familiar story of the continental European market for "corporate control." In the U.S. and the U.K.; management is hired to singularly perform one task- that of profit maximisation, or something that closely resembles this singular goal. The incentives are organised more and more to achieve this, and if performance does not live up to the benchmarks that have been projected by the army of analysts on Wall Street, then stock prices plummet until evidence emerges of a turn around or a takeover is launched. Recently, this was exactly what humbled powerful consumer products manufacturer Procter & Gamble. The benchmarks for P&G were moved upwards in tandem with the overall euphoric trend in the stock markets. Once it was announced that profit growth was not achievable in such an "old economy" sector that produced detergents and sanitary solutions, institutional investors pulled out like a herd, sending P&G shares tumbling by half. Only several months later did the stock price recover half of its losses, but at the great expense of a general management shake-up in the company.

In the "anglo-saxon" world for corporate control, companies are free to pursue buy-outs and mergers in order to expand their economies of scale, and reduce costs over the medium term, with the hopes of raising their share prices in the process. If we take our example of Procter and Gamble, then shareholders that were left holding stock that was valued at half of what it was before the announcement of lower than expected profits, could sell out to a potential external buyer of the company if they feel that the tender adequately meets their price expectations for their shares. A hostile bid for an underperforming company is a wake-up call to the management of the target, since many years invested in career paths by its managers is placed in jeopardy, thereby leading to all types of defensive tactics to ensure that it remains a going concern. This is one extreme of the market for corporate control in countries such as the U.S. and the U.K., but a mutually agreed upon merger where shares are exchanged under a predetermined formula is also a method that is used to raise shareholder value. Under a merger, duplicated functions are eliminated and size becomes a vital factor in negotiating cheaper purchases of inputs in the production process. Both of these elements raise profitability and the underlying share value of the merged company.

The Vodafone AirTouch buy-out of Mannesmann was revolutionary in the fast-emerging market of corporate control in Germany, and was a pillar transaction under which mergers and acquisitions will evolve from here on. Even some half-hearted attempts by Chancellor Gerhard Schroder to call into question the hostile nature of Vodafone AirTouch's bid in the early going, did not do much to derail the outcome. It was this one bid that did and could further change the face of the German market for "corporate control." The momentum for this to happen has been set in place, however, the all important question at this juncture is whether or not there exists a critical mass of deals of this type in order to continue the pace of change? Any lull or complacent retreat, will revert back to the traditional "stakeholder" or what has also become known as the "rhineland" model for corporate control and mergers and acquisitions in Germany.

French companies have been more aggressive in pursuing cross border acquisitions in the U.S. and in the U.K. There are about fifteen French "corporate jewels" that have the managerial know-how and product innovation, to be very effective in internationally competitive sectors. One such company that comes immediately to mind is luxury goods producer Louis Vuitton Moet Hennessy or LVMH for short. Under the leadership of entrepreneur Bernard Arnault, LVMH is aggressively acquisitive on an international scale, and has become known for its very competent management. It is companies like this that are changing the image of France, as politicians such as Lionel Jospin are forced to practice a dual policy. Domestically, Jospin is forced to preach a rhetoric that is still a remnant of the "old economy" socially-driven France, while at the same time granting a certain degree of regulatory freedom to companies such as LVMH to pursue its market operations and maximise shareholder value.

Renault's deal with Nissan Motor of Japan is one of the boldest moves in cross border mergers and acquisitions history. Does this French company have the managerial and cultural skills to succeed in turning the perennial loss-making Japanese auto company around? Despite its success or failure, the Renault and Nissan Motor deal is symbolic of the elite handful of French global companies that are not afraid to practice what most observers only preach in the new era of globalisation. It is a tribute to French management which has come full circle from the days of the Crédit Lyonnais debacle, and positions France as a "player" in the global market for corporate control. It also indicates that French companies are ready to pursue global aspirations in an aggressive way, and even goes as far as shaping the general trend towards shareholder value on continental Europe, ahead of Germany.

What of domestic acquisition targets in the French economy? Is there a Mannesmann in France that is an open target for a foreign hostile buy-out and what will be the government's reaction to such a development? The case of the French banking sector is a perfect example of the openness in France to now. Unlike the obstacles erected in the Canadian, German and even the U.K. banking markets to hostile foreign buyers, the Jospin government has opted to stay out of the local banking market and has more or less followed the Dutch model that was established in the late 1980s. Until a few years ago, the French domestic market was severely over-banked; just as is the Canadian, U.K. and German market today. When Société Générale (SG) moved to take over Banque Paribas, the Banque Nationale de Paris (BNP) joined in with the winning hostile bid for Paribas, defeating SG's initial friendly merger approach, and the market for corporate control in France was transformed overnight. What is more, the takeover of Paribas by BNP, created a balance of power vacuum on the domestic banking scene. This made it ultimately possible for U.K. based Hong Kong and Shanghai Banking Corp. (HSBC) to move into the French market via the acquisition of Crédit Commercial de France (CCF), with little opposition to the takeover. To this day, the governments of Canada, Germany and even the U.K. struggle with the thought of a foreign takeover of one of their banks, while the French banking market is well on its way to becoming one of the most efficient in Europe, if not the world.

Clearly, the market for corporate control on continental Europe is going through a change, as the globalisation of capital and the move towards one common stock exchange, creates a need for more attention to shareholder concerns than in years gone by. As the single market was supposed to create an environment for freer trade among European countries, leading to cross border buy-outs, its ironic that most European companies have been turning towards the U.S. market to acquire companies. This unprecedented move by French, German and Spanish firms to buy U.S. based companies, has contributed to the weakness in the Euro in the year 2000. It has also brought into play a new form of capital flow that currency traders need to take into serious consideration. From the early years when trade flows determined parities, to the initial stages of capital liberalisation when short term interest rates on risk free bonds drove capital flows, to the 1990s, where stock market investments shifted the global capital pool around, one must now recognise the importance of cross border mergers and acquisitions that have been behind the most recent bout of Euro weakness.

Many of the most celebrated traders and currency hedge fund managers in the 1970s and 1980s, have been caught off-guard. Their methods of trading currencies based on short term interest rate differentials have collapsed, sometimes causing painful losses in the process, while they have not been able to judge the effects of capital flows that have come about due to portfolio allocations among leading global blue-chip companies. This problem is further compounded when the new element of cross border mergers and acquisitions must be factored into the overall paradigm. The global capital pool has now become a full-fledged "free for all." Those wishing to speculate against a currency or to take long positions may never have it as easy as George Soros did when in 1992, he broke the sterling peg to the European Exchange Rate Mechanism and made somewhere around one billion pounds sterling in the process, gaining an unparalleled celebrity status throughout the entire episode and creating the foundation for his philanthropy today.

ANTI-TRUST IN A GLOBAL WORLD

The Cold War years were known for high inflation and low consumer choice, in relation to what is now available for consumers in the G•7. The initial moves to formally acknowledge the opening up of freer trade between Canada and the U.S. and the development of single market legislation within Europe, were designed to inject some badly needed competition during periods of abnormally high inflation. It was thought that the more companies that could bring their products on to domestic markets, the less would be the increases in prices throughout the Cold War years. The conception of freer trade and openness was very attractive, since it was a substitute for a re-allocation of resources away from defense spending on elaborate arms programs during this period. Strategic initiatives predominated during the 1970s and the 1980s, and the economies of the G•7 were very much tied in with the trend to keep up with the Soviet bloc countries. Much productive capacity during this period was tied up in the military-industrial complex that characterised the G•7 Gross National Product throughout this period, while trade initiatives were thought out to meet the needs of consumers.

Imports of Japanese automotive products and electronics created a massive trade deficit in the early 1980s with the U.S., but it was tolerated based on these arguments. In essence, the U.S. would provide the defense blanket to vital G•7 interests around the world, and countries such as Japan, which was a vital strategic ally, would supply consumer goods to the U.S. and hopefully keep inflation under control by providing greater competition in the market-place. Likewise, European countries were also seeking more consumer choice as inflation was just as much of a problem, and consumers even had less choice via competition than what was historically the case in North America.

The collapse of the Cold War economy left a number of "old economy" corporations vulnerable. Not only was the defense procurement industry about to dry up, but capital markets would be made far more accessible and the pool of capital much larger for expansion. Emerging market countries were slowly being tied into global markets, and those companies that were able to expand into these markets, were well positioned to drive costs down by using their newly acquired powers to bargain for lower procurement expenditures. The new era of global capital markets and freer trade held out the promise of greater price competition for all G•7 countries that were increasingly interconnected in one large market. Size became an issue for most companies that held global aspirations, as they pursued aggressive acquisitions strategies to expand market share. As the 1990s came to an end, one trend was undeniable; and that was the emergence of these very powerful "blue-chip" companies that were economically and politically more powerful than the governments of countries.

Many smaller companies that were at a disadvantage locally to larger companies that dictated the pace of procurement practices, held out great hopes for this fast emerging openness in trade and investment flows. Most of the G•7 countries' industrial sectors are organised along the lines of less than perfect competition, to outright monopolistic practices at the extreme end of the industrial spectrum. Small and mid sized companies compete against each other in markets that are more competitive, and occasionally are left to rely solely on the procurement practices of these very large and powerful blue chip companies.

The promise that was held out for the new globalisation era, quickly began to evaporate as mergers and acquisitions worked to consolidate the large corporation's grips on an ever rising market share. A market share that was ruthlessly fought for both locally as well as globally. Managerial structures were forcibly "flattened" and costs were adjusted to the new competitive pressures that began to emerge from the newly emerging markets of Asia and eastern Europe, which found themselves suddenly interconnected and plugged into the vast global market. No longer were countries such as Canada and Argentina solely relied on, in order to provide to the world natural resources, but suddenly, Russia and the countries of the former Soviet Union were now in a position to release their vast store of natural wealth onto global markets. The downward pressures on price were countered by even more companies coming together and agreeing to merge their market shares. This change in the cost structures globally, led to spiralling mergers, acquisitions and buy-outs that came to define corporate finance in the late 1990s. Never before in history, have mergers and acquisitions made the daily news headlines so frequently, as they have in the 1990s. If it wasn't Daimler Benz buying out Chrysler Corporation, then it was Citibank merging with Traveller's in the U.S. or Renault of France making a daring move into the Japanese market by buying out Nissan Motor.

Globalisation resulted in even less competition in many respects from the viewpoint of small and medium sized companies (SMEs). This became severe in the brief period of the early 1990s, when banking structures were so rigid as to not adequately provide finance capital for this sector. Yet the pressures from larger companies becoming even more larger, variously resulted in a reduction in the number of suppliers or the value of contracts awarded to this SME support sector abruptly reduced. The move towards "bigness" has truly become an anti-trust issue that should be more vigorously reviewed both within the U.S. and also in Brussels.

Cross border mergers and acquisitions have exploded in the latter half of the 1990s, making the job of the trust investigators that much more difficult any time that investigations must transcend national boundaries. Within the new era of globalisation, these organisations must be forced into accepting a coordinated approach in investigating corporate combinations. Increasingly, mergers that occur in North America are also investigated for anti-competitive practices in Brussels by the Competition Directorate, just as European mergers are now investigated in Washington D.C. by the Justice Department's Federal Trade Commission (FTC). The Competition Directorate in Brussels ruled against the $150 billion merger in the telecommunications sector that involved two large U.S. based companies; WorldCom and Sprint. In a perfect example of how the enforcement of anti-trust practices is taking shape in the new millennium, two U.S. based decisions to merge were determined to have such global repercussions in the telecoms sector, that authorities in another region of the world found it imperative to issue an official ruling against this combination. The fast-paced nature of all emerging technology sectors with their break-neck speed in innovation has overwhelmed competition that exists exclusively within local jurisdictions, such that any decisions and innovations that occur in distant geographical locations now impact local countries and economies as if the competitor itself were operating within national borders.

The much celebrated anti-trust case against software designer Microsoft that the Federal Trade Commission has been waging, also has global repercussions. The argument over an operating system and what it can and can not include from its originator, has important consequences for non-U.S. made browsers and other forms of software products that can be appended to the Windows operating system. The central focus in such a case for European countries has always been how to break into the marketing inertia that has been pre-set by Silicon Valley? If one judges the issue to be primarily one of marketing and branding power that Microsoft possesses, then the judgment rendered by the FTC is an important one that is generally good for fostering more intense competition. If Microsoft is forced to open its Windows platform to various kinds of software that is developed not only in Silicon Valley, but also in Oxford or on the French Riviera, then the playing field becomes more level and the FTC becomes a friend of the consumer. The Microsoft case, unlike telecoms and the development of the internet is far more clear cut, when placed in the context of cross border mergers and acquisitions activity. Microsoft has achieved global dominance in a more traditional manner. It has created a marketing and branding strategy that even Coca-Cola would dream of. This is in contrast to the merger which Sprint and WorldCom have negotiated, and in which the Competition Directorate in Brussels objects to in the telecoms sector. In this sector, technological moves on strictly a national level create repercussions that would normally be the preserve of the cross border acquisitions market. In this respect, all local decisions in telecoms on mergers and acquisitions strategies, immediately exact global repercussions as if the transactions themselves have been cross-border in nature at the outset. In a wired world, those sectors which have emerged as global in nature themselves, do not differentiate if mergers and acquisitions are wholly national or cross border; both national and cross border transactions now have global consequences.

As we see from these recent developments, the risk of monopoly power is now more omnipresent than it ever was in the past. The well-functioning unfettered market mechanism, which we all had hoped that a more open post Cold War era might have achieved, has been a very difficult proposition. The tendency towards global monopolies in this new high tech era can not be denied. In hindsight, one would think that the new technology and the fast emerging wired world would break down entry barriers to smaller groups. This is indeed happening through the support of venture capitalists at this very moment, however, the real danger is that all promising technologies developed through this process eventually get absorbed by the larger groups, after they are able to tender a tempting offer to sell-out, that is agreeable on behalf of both the originators of the ideas, as well as their venture capital partners and backers. In that respect, although venture capital development has been a very welcome breakthrough in the 1990s, it suffers from carrying a mentality of short termism and quick profiteering.

This brings us to the issue of global capital and financial resources, as mergers and acquisitions escalate to defend the market shares of the large mega-corporations. I mentioned that venture capital was barely existent in the early 1990s, except in Silicon Valley. It has become far more accessible in the U.S. as well as in countries such as Germany and France via government-sponsored schemes. It has yet to reach any significant impact in Canada and Japan, however, where venture capital financing has taken off up to now; it has not truly been available to the visionary longer term projects.

Many venture capitalists have preferred to operate with high tech and the internet, since the time to take a company towards an initial public offering (IPO) has been reduced from anywhere from three to five years, down to between eight and eighteen months. Every venture capitalist that is looking for returns on their equity investments above thirty percent, can not deny the allure of the high tech industry in reducing the time it takes to float off an idea into an IPO on a stock exchange. Therefore, the venture capital industry, although vital in the new economy, is far too short termist to be able to counter the emerging pressures from global mergers and acquisitions and the growing concentration, which is making the mega-corporations more powerful than the very countries in which they are domiciled and legally accountable. A large number of successful ideas that are floated on a stock exchange via an IPO, are immediately absorbed by the powerful mega high tech firms within their sectors. The true independently-minded high tech entrepreneur that is in it for the long haul, is the only insurance policy that is left to preserve a high level of competition under a period of growing global concentration.

FOREIGN DIRECT INVESTMENT

Unlike cross-border mergers and acquisitions, the formal definition of "foreign direct investment" or "direct investment" in its abbreviated form, is concerned with the physical investment process of constructing some productive asset or structure from the ground up in another country. The stereotypical foreign direct investment can be visualised as a subsidiary operation in a developing country that has been committed by a well known name brand manufacturer. For example, any automotive company in the world conducts an intricate network of productive operations around the world. Automotive parts could be sourced from as many countries as there are parts making up the end product, the automobile. It is much more efficient to move the individual parts to their respective regional assembly plants in Europe, Asia or the U.S., than it is to only assemble the final product in Detroit and then ship it to markets around the world. What used to be a common platform for producing Japanese cars in the 1970s, has evolved into the current network of parts flowing across borders to the final assembly market destination. Even the Japanese, now only export models that serve just "niche" markets around the world, such as the Lexus and Infinity brands. Most popular brands such as the Toyota Camry, or the Honda Civic, are assembled in their respective markets.

The historical interaction of trade politics and foreign direct investment was an important factor that shaped direct investment decisions during the Cold War period. The automotive industry has been the focal point for much of recent trade and direct investment developments. Just as the free trade accords negotiated in the 1980s were largely driven by the flows of automotive parts between countries, so too are foreign direct investment flows. The most famous episode of trade friction between the U.S. and Japan occurred from the late 1970s, and continued for the remainder of the 1980s, as the U.S. trade deficit reached record levels, and rising oil prices pushed the consuming American public to embrace the smaller and more efficient Japanese imports.

Then U.S. Treasury Secretary, James Baker; moved to convince his G•7 counterparts to accept a realignment of currency parities to reflect the growing trade imbalance. In one of the most celebrated eras of policy coordination and cooperation among the world's strongest economies, the Plaza and Louvre Accords were negotiated in 1985, pushing down the value of the U.S. dollar relative to other G•7 currencies for the remainder of the decade, and throughout the early years of the post Cold War period. The motivation behind this momentous event in currency management, was without a doubt the effects of Japanese automotive imports to the U.S. Prior to this, it was the formation and execution of the policies of the O.P.E.C. oil cartel, which resulted in the increased demand for smaller cars. In retrospect, these events caused the world's strongest economy to incur trade deficit after trade deficit, in a period where it was not accustomed to being a debtor to the world. Prior to the oil supply boycott by Arab countries and the execution of O.P.E.C. price increases, the U.S. never experienced a trade deficit for a lengthy period of time. Also, capital flows during the Cold War were mainly influenced by trade, without any impact from cross border mergers and acquisitions, or international portfolio allocations, which have very much become permanent features of the 1990s. In the Cold War period, trade was the only game in town, and deficits that grew beyond comfortable levels as in the case of the Japan-U.S. automotive trade, politicians were forced to mobilise corrective measures; such as moral suasion of the members of the government of the surplus country (the Carter Administration was far more belligerent towards Japanese representatives than was the Reagan Administration over the growing trade imbalance in the auto trade), outright punitive tariffs or some form of financial adjustment, as occurred under the Louvre and Plaza Accords in the mid 1980s.

What is most interesting to note from this entire episode, has been the longer term developments in foreign direct investment commitments by the Japanese, largely due to the moral suasion practiced by U.S. politicians since the late 1970s. Not only have the Japanese automotive producers made substantial investments in the U.S. and Canada, but have also been big players in the U.K. and other parts of the European continent. In fact, it is the U.K.'s concerted efforts to attract "inward investment" which has made it one of the most pre-ferred locations of Japanese, as well as U.S. based foreign direct investment. Anything from automotive parts manufacturers to high tech components com-panies, the U.K.s consistent efforts to attract investments into its depressed northern regions such as Teeside, is one of the most successful promotion cam-paigns in recent economic history. The U.K. has added a vital component to its overall domestic economic strategy. In addition to meeting the concerns and interests of the City of London, those of the inward investors ranks just as importantly.

This is most vividly illustrated by the on-going debate over the participation of the U.K. in the single European currency. The voice of the public via a referen-dum on the issue will be gauged, just as will be views of the direct investors in the northern reaches of the country. Having gone on the record in support of participation in the single currency, these investors are seeking certainty in their trade patterns destined towards the vital markets of continental Europe. When sterling is undervalued, all is well for these exporting foreign direct investors, however, when sterling is at record highs as has been the case in the early months of the new millennium, the rhetoric of the benefits of single currency participation will never cease. Many Japanese executives heading up the sub-sidiaries in the U.K. have consistently gone on record to voice their concerns should the U.K. public decide not to be a part of the project.

In the case of the U.K., it is the openness and the low tax regime which is a general draw for direct investors, however, there have been a number of other determinants of these flows historically. One such impact has been the uncer-tainty that surrounds fluctuating exchange rates. Just as in the case of interna-tional portfolio allocations, exchange rates become a very important factor in ultimately deciding to expand production beyond a firm's national borders. The problem that is associated with a direct investment in a foreign country is when profits are repatriated and consolidated. If the exchange rate moves unexpect-edly, then a profit could easily turn into a loss, and vice-versa. The yen-dollar

parity has seen a significant fluctuation over the past twenty years. This relationship between two of the most important G•7 currencies is notorious for
being difficult to predict. Consequently, when trade rhetoric peaks in Congress,
the yen rises abruptly and sometimes dramatically. There were at least three
circumstances in the 1990s, where the swings in the dollar-yen parity exceeded
fifty percent per annum. Under these sets of conditions, Japanese automotive
direct investments in the U.S. are under the spotlight, as profits made in the
U.S. may turn into a loss when stated in yen terms for local accounting customs. If the yen rises by fifty percent in one year relative to the dollar, then an
increase of even thirty percent in U.S. profits will be translated into a net loss
on manufacturing operations there. Likewise, if Japanese transplant companies
that have located in the local U.K. economy to export a high proportion of their
production to the European continent are faced with severely overvalued sterling conditions, then profitability is offset by a loss of market share due to the
high and uncompetitive sterling denominated exports.

Reading the daily financial press, one can not help but to notice the countless
stories about how unwieldy currency swings have ultimately caused a net loss,
or a net decrease in profits, just when a direct investment was considered to be
a good strategy based on servicing and preserving important foreign markets by
deciding to establish a physical presence in these markets. Countries with a
high proportion of manufacturing companies relative to service companies have
always promoted greater exchange rate stability. On numerous occasions, the
French and the Germans, have always stood in favour of limited exchange rate
fluctuations, in order to assist the export and direct investment interests of their
manufacturing companies. This is not the case with the U.S. and the "Anglo-
saxon" bloc of countries that have been more or less indifferent to any attempts
to limit currency fluctuations. In the U.K., the Confederation of British
Industry, the arm that represents the interests of British manufacturers has been
openly critical of the high levels of sterling, however, the Bank of England has
continually refused to reduce base rates which are believed to be supporting the
high levels of the currency. Under such circumstances, given that the U.K. is
now more a service economy than it is an industrial one; the Bank of England
is poised to pay more attention to the pressures of inflation in the services, than
it is to the problems that manufacturers are having in servicing their traditional
export markets. Services rule in the U.K., and the Confederation of British
Industry knows this, thereby promoting more vigorously than ever the need for
U.K. producers to engage themselves in direct investments abroad in order to
escape this unfriendly exchange rate regime. Consequently, this trend has been
on the increase to the extent that the manufacturing sector has gone a long way
in adjusting to the strong pound sterling. Manufacturers have been engaged in a
campaign to preserve their foreign markets by themselves establishing a foreign direct presence in these vital markets. One can go as far as stating that this

transformation in the U.K. manufacturing base has already been accomplished, and that from here on it has become impervious to the high levels of the domestic currency.

From many empirical investigations into foreign direct investment flows, including this author's, it can safely be assumed that corporations that engage in this activity are more motivated based on financial uncertainties such as the foreign exchange effect, than they are purely on attempts to arbitrage tax rates. My own view is that companies on average, are not motivated by lower tax rates in deciding where to build a plant. What seem to be the over-riding factors, have more to do with the size of market share, and most importantly, the financial conditions that surround the decision to break out of the domestic marketplace. Financial conditions have to do with such issues as currency convertibility; how independent and transparent monetary policy and the central bank are; and the nature of the fluctuations in the currency parities, as discussed above. What good is it if profits can not be repatriated out of a country? This factor has to a great extent held back the development of many newly-emerging countries in central Europe. The lack of convertibility prospects in Slovenia, Croatia, Romania and Bulgaria has held back foreign direct investments, and even worse has re-directed them to more friendlier climates in Latin America and Asia. Therefore, it is the financial factors that often determine the direction of foreign direct investment flows, especially within the G•7.

DEVELOPING TO EMERGING MARKETS

During the years of the Cold War, the fight for ideological supremacy between the Communist bloc and the Western "capitalist" countries led by the U.S., was waged in "developing countries," as both factions moved to bribe them into becoming absorbed within their respective sphere of influence. Most notably, countries such as Syria, Cuba and the central European countries of Poland, Czechoslovakia and Hungary, were offered very generous support programs for developing an industrial base, as well as very favourable oil prices by the Soviet Union. Likewise, countries within the western "capitalist" bloc such as Israel and Egypt, as well as most European NATO members were offered very generous economic development programs, usually led by U.S. military spending on various forms of local projects and procurement.

The annual aid to Israel and Egypt exceeded some seven billion dollars throughout the 1980s, which in turn created a steady flow of orders to the U.S. defense industry for military aircraft and weaponry. These so called "developing" countries were approached from an ideological perspective throughout the Cold War by the two competing sides. The U.S. led western bloc was not too concerned whether their allies in the developing world fully adopted a free market system, and in many respects ended up supporting various forms of dictatorships in Latin and South America, so as to deter any moves that would send these countries into the Soviet bloc. What defined these countries throughout this period was their politics in relation to the two competing blocs, and not their economics.

This changed when the Berlin Wall collapsed and the bi-polar system of the Cold War became absorbed in the globalisation system. Suddenly, free markets became more transparent and efficient the further the decade of the 1990s progressed, and the once developing countries that were fed inefficient aid from the two competing ideological blocs, now became absorbed in various degrees into the single global marketplace. Gone were the tolerance levels of the former Soviet Union and the U.S., where inept dictators in Syria and Argentina were kept in power despite years of economic neglect and poor performance. These countries were now being re-defined as "emerging markets" that would eventually become absorbed in the new system of "globalisation." There would from here on be an informal ranking ranging from the advanced G•7 economies that set most of the market and consumer trends throughout the world, to the second tier members of the OECD which were not subjected to any degree of central planning prior to the 1990s as well as the "tiger" economies of South Korea, Thailand and Malaysia which displayed an ability to grow fast, down the scale to those countries that were part of the former Soviet Union and which had to first get accustomed to what a transparent market actually was.

The attitudes towards this third tier of countries was very different under the two systems of the Cold War economy and that of globalisation. Under the former, political decisions were the ultimate determinants of any resource mobilisations. If the U.S. needed the loyalty of both Egypt and Israel for its regional strategic and military operations within the western Middle East or northwest Africa, then the yearly price tag was to be set at around seven billion dollars. If the former Soviet Union needed a strategic regional partner in the Middle East, it proceeded to send billions of scarce resources to Syria. Geopolitical and strategic goals of the two opposing sides came first, whereas the inefficient economic allocations used to buy loyalty were a distant second consideration.

In the new system of globalised efficient markets, backed by the speed and promise of constantly evolving technological developments, the second and third tier economies that are now defined as "emerging markets" are largely devoid of any direct political and strategic meddling. (Although many have argued that the new globalisation system is largely a form of "Americanisation")

What used to be a vital strategic interest under the Cold War system, is now only valuable if it meets the economic requirements of the global investor class. Be it foreign direct investors, portfolio fund managers or cross border acquirors of companies, the most important thing now is that the fiscal, monetary and political policies become investor-friendly within these newly emerging markets. Policies such as balanced budgets, or even better still, budgets that are in surplus, together with independent central banks that are not influenced by elected politicians, are now the minimal requirements that global investors look to in judging the attractiveness of emerging markets.

In essence, developing countries under the old Cold War system, have gone from being in a "push" type of investment climate, to the "pull" that exists under globalisation. In the former, it was governments or states which decided if a certain country or region was worthy of economic or financial support, whereas in the latter, it is now the actions of private decision makers that are constantly scrutinizing if a certain country is worthy of having investment flow inwards. More than ever, these private investors have become the developers of these emerging countries. The policy which is central in determining if money flows towards a certain country, is that country's track record in behaving appropriately when the time comes to take the money home. Repatriation of capital combined with currency convertibility are two fundamental aspects of bringing an emerging market country into the single global market. If these two fundamental aspects are absent, then the country will never attract this growing pool of private international capital, but may only be relegated into negotiating the occasional IMF or World Bank sponsored loan.

Political and geo-strategic decisions have succumbed to private investment decisions globally in the 1990s. The growing power of international capital flows is defining what is and what is not acceptable in the form of local policies. More than ever before, national parliaments and legislatures are being dictated to by this growing global constituency of mobile and powerful investors. Despite this power, there still remain several hold-outs and rogue governments that refuse to play by the rules of the new game. Countries such as Serbia, Zimbabwe and North Korea continue to pine for the former system when they were in some form of regional control, both politically and economically. North Korea has recently begun to open up to better relations with South Korea, hence it will be scrutinized very closely by this powerful and mobile pool of global capital, and as soon as investors become convinced of its motives, then they will aggressively begin to search for attractive opportunities within the country. The population of North Korea will benefit from commitments to various forms of projects and efforts at modernisation. India and Pakistan also belong within this category of being transition economies. They were always against aggressive foreign investors dictating the terms of their engagement domestically, but recently, there has been a proliferation of high technology companies that have begun to exploit India's expertise in software and design.

The countries of the Balkans have been the most interesting to watch during this period of system transformation. Some have embraced the new system, yet others remain way behind and are still mourning the old Cold War state of Yugoslavia both openly as well as secretly. The northern most alpine Republic of Slovenia has been ready for accession to the European Union, while Croatia is winning in its struggle to make its country attractive to the international pool of capital, in the post Tudman era. However, the effort stops at the border of Serbia, which under Slobodan Milosevic, remains opposed to openness with this powerful pool of international investment capital. The recent moves by NATO, to bomb Belgrade in order to force an independent Kosovo, is a poisonous outcome to any hopes of reversing the flow of international investment. In this case, it goes to show that a country that is as internationally isolated as is Serbia at this time, must rely on an underground black market economy to ensure that a continuous functioning of the local economy continues. This functioning and allocation of resources is accomplished through the black market and channels of organised crime, and is performed both informally and inefficiently. Only when Serbia decides that it is in its best interest to plug into this global power pool of capital, will it gain formality, efficiency and a more prosperous country. To now, the political leadership is still struggling with this newly emerging private balance of global power.

The countries that made up the former Yugoslavia, have all had varying degrees of success in the new global economy. After going through a difficult transition and war, only Slovenia has been recognised as an early candidate to join the European common market. Croatia has made progress and has tried very hard to integrate into the global marketplace, but has a long way to go in preparing its management that has become entrenched in former state-owned enterprises, which have been recently privatised. Both the northern two republics of the former Yugoslavia; Croatia and Slovenia, seem as though they will make it into the new system of globalisation, but for Croatia the transition will be a difficult one. Interestingly, these two republics in the old Yugoslavia, were also providing most of the industrial infrastructure and productivity during the Cold War era when the region was unified into one state.

The remaining former republics of Bosnia and Hercegonia and Macedonia, have had the most difficulty in the transition period of the 1990s. Macedonia is a landlocked agricultural country at the very south end of the former

Yugoslavia, and has been subjected to a massive refugee problem from the recent NATO campaign in Kosovo. To make matters worse, Macedonia has been an historic enemy with Greece to the south and has had difficult relations with Albania that borders it to the west. Prior to the NATO bombing campaign, it struggled with finding a niche to trade in, and was mainly restricted to an agrarian type of economy with little prospect of developing any industrial advantages. The global economy may bring bright prospects in terms of creating some sort of service economy base in the country, which may move its reliance away from agriculture over time.

In the case of Bosnia and Hercegovina; the Dayton Peace Plan negotiated by former Secretary of State Warren Christopher, attempted to artificially keep the three factions of Serbs, Croats and Muslims together in one democratic country. The reality is that Bosnia is economically split, with Croatia supplying trade to the Bosnian Croat region, while the Serbs are aiding the trade of Republika Srpska, the Serb-controlled region. Bosnian economic activity is more or less determined along this pattern of trade and investment currently. Bosnia is also a black market-driven country that contains an increasingly large dispersion in wealth among its citizens. Black market gains are the driving force behind the country, while official U.S. and EU influence try very hard to bring its economy into the global mainstream, with little success up to now. Bosnia is also a country that yearns for the old system, where politicians affect the allocation of resources and economic activity, and where private investors play a very limited role. Under such a situation, globalisation as defined by the growing private pool of mobile capital, can affect Bosnia only if substantial guarantees are offered to any investors by organisations like the World Bank or the European Bank for Reconstruction and Development (EBRD).

Even among the advanced economies of the G•7, there exist some countries that are more prepared for globalisation than others. The outcome that has become the most prevalent over the 1990s has been the favourable and quick transition experienced in the Anglo-Saxon countries of the U.S., U.K. and Canada. The best transition made for private investors has been by the U.S. and the U.K., while Canada has had a difficult landing in the early years of the decade. The U.S. has led the way with productivity gains via the accelerating growth in its high tech and venture capital base. This has pushed up the potential growth in G.N.P. and has resulted in lower inflation and interest rates, creating an environment that is favourable for a higher budget surplus. This quick change has caught the imagination of all types of foreign investment, as they can not get enough exposure to the U.S. Likewise, in the case of the U.K. the ease of repatriating capital and investment has always attracted foreign investment into the country. This attraction is what continually causes havoc with U.K. based exporters, as they struggle with an overvalued pound sterling pushed up by foreign investors seeking exposure to the U.K. economy and currency.

The continental European countries making up the G•7, such as France, Germany and Italy, have had a more difficult transition to a regime governed by private capital flows and global investment. Firstly, in the case of Germany, the country's corporate sector has always been organised in accordance to what has become termed as the "rhineland model." Under this system, there was a partnership between management, shareholders and labour unions. Labour unions always had a seat on the Supervisory Board, and management always played a mediation role in serving a "middle-ground" between the three levels of competing interests. Managers were never required to be short-termist and to maximise profits and shareholder values in the process. Meanwhile, the banking and insurance establishment always held some form of substantial shareholding in major conglomerate companies like Mannesmann, Bayer or Siemens. At the same time, individual shareholders were expected not to "rock the boat" at yearly meetings, as long as profit levels were deemed to be acceptable in a given company.

France was also organised along similar patterns as was German industry, except that it had a substantially larger civil service. During the Cold War period, French industries were usually managed by political appointees, who in their own right were extremely non-commercial in orientation and plain incompetent at managing any enterprise. Scandals surrounding oil company Elf Aquitaine, and the classic failure of Crédit Lyonnais, were cases in point. The end of the Cold War required a radical transformation of this culture of cronyism and appointments, if French industry was to flourish under the new era. State controlled companies had to sell-off their holdings, privatise the companies and de-commission conglomerate companies. The process entailed a radical reorganisation of French management culture, as well as the general culture of France itself.

In the case of Italy, the transformation would also be difficult. Gone were the days when the large family-controlled industries could rely on state hand-outs if they failed to make a profit in a given year of operation. The classic case of the Agnelli-controlled Fiat automotive empire, was forced to sell-off all non-core subsidiaries and to bring in U.S. executive talent to compete in the new world. Also, the byzantine financial system had to go through a massive merger and acquisition program, in order to prepare for the global investment market, and to get ready for Italy's participation in the single European currency program. Also, the ineffective Milan Bourse was privatised, and reorganised so as to become more responsive to technology investors, both locally and globally. The transition was enormously difficult, and Italy only began to achieve some noticeable gains in the final year of the 1990s.

By contrast, the anglo-saxon grouping of countries already had corporations and companies organised along short-term goals. Those that issued stock were required to report on a quarterly basis their forecasted and actual profits. They were not organised in partnership with labour unions, and the goal of management was to maximise profits and to increasingly mind the share price of their companies. More and more, management was remunerated by a combination of fixed pay and stock options, and these would only rise in value if the enterprise was deemed as being in good hands. The further the 1990s progressed, the greater was the emphasis on stock options and management of share prices. Increasingly, share buy-backs would become a regular feature of management's program to maintain corporate value under conditions of rising efficiencies.

The dynamic surrounding the evolution of the global market was such as to thrust all of the G•7 members, regardless of which countries were ready for change or not, into the forefront as the main promoters of globalisation. If one believed in a market style of economy, then there was no room for a "balanced" approach in the new system of globalisation. Much to the grief of continental European members of the G•7, the inertia created by the fast paced changes in technology and the internet, caused abrupt changes that local populations were more or less forced to accept. For instance, the rise of profit maximising behaviour on the part of corporate managers was something that workers in Germany and in France were not accustomed to. Also, the countless attempts at reforming the French Civil service into an environment that is more friendly towards private investors, has resulted in vigorous attempts to halt the progress of the global system within France by its many unions. Many socially-organised countries that were inward-looking during the Cold War, have found it a very difficult time throughout the 1990s.

The G•7 as a whole is now much more marketised and connected to each other through the global marketplace, than it was ever before. During the Cold War period, the advanced industrialised countries that were part of the G•7, were bound to each other via strictly financial markets; the most obvious of which was the foreign exchange market. Even stock markets during this time were not in a position to be opened to foreign investors from other G•7 countries, and consumer banking products were strictly regulated by domestic legislation with plenty of restrictions. What is more, product markets were inefficient and only very few commodities could have been called truly global in nature. What comes to mind immediately is the oil spot price market that long existed in Rotterdam, and which was an authoritative guide and signal as to the conditions in the global oil markets. Likewise, the markets for some precious metals such as gold, silver and platinum were also sufficiently globalised, and any movement in local prices for these commodities was immediately transmitted to mines around the world.

Under the new system of globalisation, supported through the "internet economy," even the minutest consumer items are now sufficiently globalised and commoditised, as a heightened level of competition around the world ensures a fair price. If a radiator for a BMW costs three times more than what a local dealer in Germany or Belgium is selling the product, then an owner living in the midwest of the U.S. can now simply order it over the internet, and bypass the locally inefficient pricing structure. Likewise, if a Ford Mustang owner in the south of France needs a new set of tail-lights, and the local garage does not stock the item, she may bypass the local market completely by ordering the product through the internet from a U.S. parts dealer, or directly from the Ford Motor Company's website. By tying consumer products into the world marketplace, the new system is ensuring that there will always be a natural hedge against inflation. The new system will also ensure that any pricing differentials will be arbitraged away, much to the benefit of consumers in higher cost countries.

Canada, Germany, France and Italy have been forced to make a very painful adjustment to the new system, and at a great sacrifice to their social infrastructures and institutions to now. The adoption of a full-fledged global market has come a little easier in the U.K., and has been completely endorsed and embraced by the dynamism of the U.S. economy. The second tier countries like Ireland, Finland, Brazil and Argentina, have also embraced the new system at a great cost of adjustment locally. The newly-emerging markets of central Europe and Asia have had to adjust with the greatest of difficulty from their formerly centrally-planned economies. After a decade in the new system, many are still struggling with the way in which they have become intertwined into the new global market. There are several winners in this respect and these include; Slovenia, Poland, Turkey, Hungary, the Czech Republic, Thailand, Malaysia and Argentina, while the status of others has been in suspense, including countries such as Croatia, Macedonia, Bulgaria, Romania, Slovakia, Russia and the Ukraine, while those that are resisting the global market or the power of private and institutional investors, include Serbia, Algeria, Libya, Colombia and Indonesia.

A common characteristic shared by those emerging market countries that have embraced the global market system now, is that they were economically organised under a system of some sort of market historically. Many central European countries that were part of the Austro-Hungarian empire prior to the advent of the Cold War system, have seen a successful transformation to globalisation. Also, countries that had stock exchanges a century ago, are well ahead in the new system. All of the central European countries mentioned above, including Croatia, had some sort of stock exchange and trading of equities prior to the Cold War. In Turkey, the equity culture is rampant, as the country has effectively used centuries of stock market culture, in embracing a modern economy that is at the forefront of its application to become a member of the European Union. It is these historical attributes of countries and remnants of previous experiments with a market system, which may determine the ultimate success or failure within the system of globalisation. Having relied on political decisions from the state, many countries are just unable to come to terms with the main pillars of the new system; the private decisions of investors backed by the power of global capital and high technology.

VENTURE CAPITAL

Prior to the mid 1990s, venture capital was a term that was restricted to several maverick investors on Wall Street. These investors were usually classified as "Angels" in the strict sense that they started a company (a venture) sometime in the past, and were subsequently bought out by a larger firm (usually a corporation), cashing in several million dollars in the process. In short, Angels were successful entrepreneurs that now sit on a huge pile of cash after successfully selling out their operations to other interested parties. What distinguishes Angels, is that they are very unlike today's MBA-trained, institutionalised managers of huge venture capital funds. Angels were also hands-on operators of businesses that more often than not, were not schooled formally in any university, let alone an ivy-league MBA program.

Many Angel venture capitalists needed to be involved in growing companies from the start up phase, since this was their true love in life. They usually knew each other in cities like New York, and went on occasionally to pool their risk capital together in a larger fund that would invest in start up companies that they believed in. The entire process was very informal, and what distinguished these investors was the successes that they had in starting up, then running and ultimately selling out their own companies. What was also interesting is that this form of risk capital was exclusively created in the U.S. Among other G•7 countries, venture capital was a foreign subject, where many still to this day struggle with it. Venture capital is also a cultural term, in that successful private investors are willing to put up some of their money and back an idea, or back a successful management team with some type of track record or reputation.

This was unheard of in countries like Canada, and the continental European countries. In Germany, there was a very strong small and medium sized company sector called the "Mittelstand" that was mainly a family unit of production that spanned many generations. These Mittelstand were notoriously conservative and refused to allow outside managers, even if their immediate family was neither interested nor qualified to continue with the business. Moreover, they refused to sell the family operation to any outsiders, or to any other companies within Germany. They provided most of the export earnings of Germany, and produced high quality engineering products that were no match in global markets, even during the period of the Cold War.

Like Germany's Mittelstand, Italy has produced the fashion equivalent. Companies organised in a family type model included some of the best known name brands today. Clothing and fashion retailer, Bennetton is notorious for its closed family structure, while its success internationally grew in prominence. Likewise, most Italian fashion companies such as Fendi, Bulgari and Gucci, were all family controlled businesses that rose to international prominence and carved out a very successful and profitable niche. In the automotive area, there was the family-operated Ferrari; probably one of the most celebrated name brands of luxury and performance in the world today. Along with Ferrari engineering, came the design of Pininfarina, who collaborated with the great Enzo Ferrari, and whose operation today run by heir Sergio Pininfarina, employs over one thousand automotive designers near Turin, and which counts the "big 3" U.S. automakers as clients. Also, auto designer "ItalDesign" is a family-run business that has become very successful and which most recently raised capital in Milan via an initial public offering. Unlike the U.S. model that was in search of "backable ideas" and "backable managements," the European model was more closed in the sense that extended family groups gathered together and raised financing to launch their companies. In this sense, the venture capital in Europe was culturally defined in a less transparent framework, compared with the open and meritocratic U.S. approach.

The Canadian experience with venture capital is nothing short of disastrous. Canada's venture capital stock exchange located in Vancouver, was always associated with mining ventures with some ninety-eight percent of listings failing. Under this style of framework, there was very little scope for developing a family business as in the case of both Italy and Germany's experiences, and those family businesses that were developed usually benefitted from some kind of extraordinary event or luck. The problems associated with the banking practices of the large banks in Canada are well documented. Aside from their traditional administrative approaches to lending based on the security of residential real estate, their allocations to small and medium sized companies only increased in the latter half of the 1990s, after large companies moved to meet their financing needs via the buoyant stock markets, hence not requiring the services of the large banks.

The concept of venture capital has taken off in the 1990s. Never before has venture capital become so mainstream, as it has in the era of globalisation and technological innovation. In the U.S., the venture capitalist has evolved from the informal Wall Street based entrepreneur that has successfully sold off his business, to a professionally designated technocrat that specialises in screening some three to ten business plan submissions every day. Smaller informal pools of capital have also been opened up by large pension funds in the U.S. By promising rates of return substantially higher than average investments, funds such as Advent in the U.S. and 3i in the U.K., have successfully raised billions of dollars to invest in projects. Such funds have evolved into mega-structured banking operations that have raided M.B.A. schools for talent. No longer is risk capital disbursed based on the good feelings of those that have successfully "cashed-out," but now there is a far more formal and mechanical way of investing risk capital. A rigorous adherence to ratios and financial analysis of business plans is now the *modus operandi* of the large venture capital funds.

Further, what used to be a time frame of three to five years, has been reduced to one year or less for venture capital commitments to new companies. The frenzy of internet company floatations and high tech initial public offerings in the 1990s has appealed to venture capitalists' sense of greed. Every venture capitalist knows that from a portfolio of ten investments, there could be one that becomes a true "home run," whereby a floatation on a stock exchange will return a winfall that will offset many of the investments that have either failed or not lived up to expectations. Therefore, the more certain the environment for an initial public offering (IPO) and the easier that the market for IPOs becomes, the better-off are venture capitalists under such conditions. This is exactly the type of environment that evolved in the latter half of the 1990s in the U.S. as the internet "dot.com" craze was gathering momentum. Throughout the process, investors were willing to invest in IPOs with no history or track record whatsoever. There was so much surplus cash, that money was being thrown at anything that was brought to the market; usually after only nine months of founding the company and attracting an early round of financing from the venture capital community. Gone were the days of venture capital being some form of "patient capital" that was committed to an investee for a minimum of three years.

In continental European countries, a phenomenon was also developing. This was the creation of venture capital or junior company stock exchanges that specialised in raising equity capital via an initial public offering. In Germany, the Neuer Markt was formed and in Brussels it was the EASDAQ, while in Paris the small venture capital community was behind the Nouveau Marché. Moreover, there are now junior company exchanges that were also formed in

Milan and in Madrid, in addition to the multitude of plans to expand small company markets to the emerging countries of central Europe. Now, more than ever before, Europe was attractively positioned to attract small companies that were searching for equity risk capital. In many ways, the development of the venture market in Europe has become directly competitive with New York, Boston and Silicon Valley. Many venture capitalists have commented that the regulations for floating on a European exchange are often less onerous than are the listing rules on the NASDAQ in New York.

In the case of Germany, the Schroder government has moved very aggressively in order to catch up with the U.S. They have gone as far as providing generous state guarantees to investors who would like to put up capital for investments in start-ups, completely by-passing the traditional family-organised Mittelstand sector. Likewise, the Jospin government in France has come to terms with the fact that they must maintain a pace with financial developments in Europe, especially if Germany has begun to aggressively promote the concept.

Further, the large New York money-centre banks such as Chase Manhattan and Citigroup have joined in on the 1990s venture capital boom, except that the term that has become more fashionable is "private equity." Often, venture capital and private equity are grouped together, yet they really have very little in common. Private equity is a term that defines a re-allocation of a company's capital structure. When a venture capital fund engages in a "private equity" deal, it usually backs a management buy-out of a company or a division that no longer fits in with the broader strategic goals of the group. Usually in such a deal, the management is well known in a particular sector and has a stellar reputation. There are also situations where a management buy-in occurs. This could be the case in successions where a leading manager or group of managers is backed to take a stake in a leading company. Direct loans may also be extended for these situations in the hopes that the private equity firm will cash out via an IPO, or some sort of dividend or buy-back. In short, the private equity fund provides a short term class of funding, so that the capital structure can be reformed to take better account of the new situation that the firm in question finds itself in.

By contrast, venture capital is a development concept. It is strictly reserved for start-ups, or backing new ideas or well respected managers that plan to strike out on their own. Historically, venture capital was far the more risky concept, and was committed for much longer periods of time than was private equity. In the case of the New York money-centre banks that are getting involved in venture capital and private equity, it is more the latter form of financing that they are preferring to engage themselves in. Venture capital deals are restricted to the fast-paced high tech and internet sectors, where an IPO can be floated within one year. The evidence over 1999 has been convincing, as the best divisional performers on a profitability measure within the money-centre commercial banks and investment banks, has been the private equity areas. Most large commercial banks have named their private equity divisions; "...Capital Partners" with a mandate to exploit the fastest returns available in what is fast becoming the trendy high tech sector.

German auto maker BMW's disastrous foray into U.K. auto production and assembly by acquiring Rover group, is a perfect example on how a private equity fund was called in to assist in the disposal of the loss making subsidiary. In this case, Alchemy Partners private equity fund based in London, was approached by the management of BMW to buy its Rover subsidiary. However, an outcry by the labour unions against Alchemy's plans to break up the company into its most profitable unit, the production of the MG sports cars and the sale of Land Rover to Ford Motor Company, resulted in a competing bid to surface that was led by the former management of Rover, and which was informally backed by the labour government of Tony Blair. The intention all along was to save the high volume production of Rover cars in the UK, and to preserve most of the jobs associated with this activity. Alchemy Partners planned to phase out high volume automotive production completely, leaving just the niche production of the MG brand.

What Alchemy Partners was called in to do was in no way connected with venture capital. It did not provide any risk capital to back a new idea, nor did it finance any expansion plans. Its role was simply to take a non-profitable subsidiary of BMW away and strip it of its unattractive parts; in this case high volume automotive production, and sell-off the remaining high profit margin activities at more than what it would pay BMW. In essence, BMW was discounting the restructuring activity in the price that it would be charging Alchemy, leaving the difficult decisions to the private equity group. The transaction was similar to a management buy-out of a division, except that Alchemy Partners was the temporary management company of Rover cars.

Rover was eventually bought out by a more politically correct consortium of investors that included some previous Rover executives, with the full intention of preserving high volume production in the U.K. Ultimately, BMW ended up selling Rover for a symbolic ten pounds sterling to the new Phoenix Consortium. This is a case that would have been far too political for a private equity group to manage, and any implementation of its mandate would have brought immense political repercussions for the labour government. In this respect, private equity involves very complicated financial engineering, and reallocates the structure of a target's balance sheet in the process, usually providing equity financing to replace some forms of temporary bank lending to the principals of the transaction. Private equity means exactly what the name implies; equity risk capital that is not derived from a public offering of stock and that is extended for a variety of reasons to companies that are already in a mature phase of their life, wishing to restructure their operations. Venture capital is equity risk capital that backs solid managerial talent with an innovative idea and is usually reserved to define a start-up company.

Looking back at the Cold War era, it was private equity that was the most active form of investment throughout the 1980s. Having experimented with a less than optimal allocation between debt and equity throughout the 1970s, corporate stock prices on Wall Street were depressed for many years to come. In the midst of major macroeconomic shocks that saw a rapid rise in oil prices, monetary inflation and wage and price controls during the Nixon years, not to mention the climax of the ending of the Viet Nam war, corporate America mobilised its capital-raising activity by issuing an over-supply of stock, depressing share prices in the process. Meanwhile, various financial theories proposed by finance Professor Merton Miller and economist Franco Modigliani, and taught extensively to new managers in emerging MBA programs throughout the U.S. formed a new paradigm for corporate finance.

Management needed to do everything in order to raise share prices, and the oversupply of float issued in the turbulent 1970s had to be restructured and bought back. Corporations were advised to re-leverage their balance sheets in order to raise their shareholder values, and this is exactly what happened throughout the 1980s. The process for re-engineering the balance sheets of companies was a very early form of private equity, or a form of reverse private equity to be more precise. The move to re-leverage balance sheets of corporations climaxed in the late 1980s, as specialist buy-out funds emerged on the scene on Wall Street. The most celebrated of these was Kohlberg, Kravis, Roberts (KKR), lead by financier Henry Kravis which revolutionised the leveraged buy-out, along with Michael Milken of Drexel Burnham Lambert, who promoted the development of the high yield bond market; a vital financing mechanism that allowed corporations to re-leverage their balance sheets in the late 1980s and in the process raise shareholder value.

Venture capital in the 1970s and in the 1980s was informal and restricted to the successful entrepreneurs that "cashed-out" from their own companies successfully. The transition to the system of globalisation in the 1990s resulted in dramatic growth in venture capital funds driven by new opportunities that were being created in the internet and high tech sectors. Ideas were now becoming more "bankable" and widely accepted, especially those that had a basis in high technology, while the re-allocative function that private equity delivers to corporate business development executives has remained relatively constant from its inaugural period in the latter half of the 1980s. Private equity, in this respect, has transcended the shift in systems, extending its reach from the 1980s well into the new era of globalisation. The venture capital market, on the other hand, has not been so stable, as the advent of spectacular returns on internet and high tech investments in the latter half of the 1990s, has created a real boom in new professionally managed funds that were looking to take advantage of this trend.

VENTURE CAPITAL IN 90 DAYS

There are few authentic venture capitalists remaining in the G•7. One of these rare few that I got to know is an American living in Zagreb, Croatia, named Scott Ferguson. Not only is Mr. Ferguson a venture capitalist, he is also keenly interested in economic development. Although he was the first professional manager of a venture capital fund in Croatia promoted by the U.S. Treasury, his attempts to raise money for his own newly-established "Xvest" fund has been a rough going up to now. Despite the fact that there is a surplus of money available within the G•7, witnessed by the proliferation of funds everywhere of every shape and size, investors have been frightened by two factors, one of which has much to do with the political instability of the Balkans region. The less obvious impediment affecting the fund raising efforts of the Xvest Fund, have been the perceived lack of "dot.com" and high tech companies located in a country like Croatia. A brief glance at the potential Xvest portfolio of investee companies presents a widely diversified grouping, ranging from leading luxury products producers that service the European duty free market, to newly-devised plans to create revolutionary de-mining machines for this war-ravaged region. According to Mr. Ferguson, each of the investees are a true gem, in that they can already show a profitable track record of several years; a ready export market in continental Europe and a management team that has displayed a high degree of flexibility, having to navigate business affairs through several war-ravaged years in the early 1990s.

Being a traditional venture capital fund within an emerging market country, the Xvest fund must not only navigate around the complacency of G•7 investors by virtue of the fact that it is not predominantly a high tech fund, but also must be alert to the possibility of exchange controls within Croatia not to mention political instability. However, the track record of potential investees is undisputed, having already weathered many years of turmoil, war and general instability, not to mention an inept and illiquid domestic banking system. More specifically, the best companies within an emerging market environment such as Croatia must be risk managers, as much as they are producers of products. One of the most compelling risks that any entrepreneur faces, is the existence of a punitive banking system. During the height of the Balkan war, it was commonplace to encounter situations where small and medium sized enterprises were forced to pay in excess of fifty percent on loans in duration of less than a year. During peaceful times, the situation is no better, since overdraft and borrowing rates are commonly in excess of twenty percent. Entrepreneurs tend to work around the banking system, preferring to deal with supplier credits and by using hard currency from export earnings. Xvest fund investees are very adept at using foreign exchange earnings to finance production, investment and expansion. Most have revenues in excess of eighty percent that are sourced from exports to countries such as Austria, Italy and Germany. Expansion plans of these investees are proportional to the cash-flows generated from export earnings. In essence, the job of the venture capitalist is academic to a certain extent. With a proven management adept at navigating through a diverse array of crises, expansion capital provided would result in a projected rate of return in excess of thirty percent on a majority of investments in these local companies. This may not be to the liking of the "dot.com" investors, but it is acceptable to investors wishing for exposure within a more traditional grouping of sectors and companies.

Therefore, what is wrong with contemporary G•7 based venture capitalists, when an uncrowded and untapped pipeline of exceptional investees goes unrecognised? Is it that these perceptions of "old economy" investments are shunned in general, or is it just specific to the emerging economy risk scenario, that Croatia is very much a part of? Since Croatian "blue-chip" stocks such as pharmaceutical group Pliva and Zagrebacka Banka have attracted their fair share of German, Italian and Austrian institutional funds, it can not be the case that country risk is a hindrance to interested investors. No, its issue is not the geographical location of the Xvest fund, but a general disinterest among investors in more traditional investments, hence longer term commitments to the investees themselves. If venture capital has become such a short term exercise; limited to the "dot.com" investment, in the hopes that a quick initial public offering (IPO) can be flipped within a time horizon of less than one year, then this form of investment becomes nothing more than an activity fostering a "bubble" or "casino" style of economy.

Certainly, there are some justifications for entering into an IPO in less than one year for certain types of investments, but recent trends are beginning to indicate that this is quickly being accepted as the norm for venture capital investments. The days of patient capital seem to be long gone, and as with the experience with the Xvest fund, investors seem only to be interested in some form of internet or high technology investment, solely based on the spectacular returns in which a quick exit on the stock market can bring. If your story is not high tech, there is no money available for your investees, and it seems that if the high tech and internet bubble bursts, all investments will dry up without much shifting of capital towards more traditional sectors, despite the fact that returns could still be had in excess of thirty percent. The large institutions that raise money for venture capital funds, really are not acting as venture capitalists as their exit horizons become more short term.

The natural structural changes in the era of globalisation that brought accelerated competition and opened up trade; supported by rapid communication and technological change, worked to reduce inflationary expectations and bring about disinflation in most sectors and outright deflation in some others. Investors and savers began a frantic search for returns, releasing funds into blue-chip stocks. In fact, throughout the 1990s, this dynamic has created unprecedented wealth for stock holders and owners of private companies, thereby exacerbating their dilemmas even further, until a situation of too much money chasing too few adequate returns surfaced and which continues to be the case until this very day. In short, there is a lot of wealth created in the 1990s and there is a lot of money circulating looking for adequate rates of return. After the crises in the emerging markets which began in Asia and spread to the Russian default in 1998, the situation whereby few acceptable investment channels existed became even more apparent. By stripping out emerging market investments after the multitude of defaults, investors were relegated to chasing fewer and fewer safe G•7 based paper investments. Moreover, as most of these industrially advanced economies were moving to surplus fiscal positions, less risk-free bonds were being issued for investment portfolios. Furthermore, for every one private company that was announcing a sell-off, there were usually between ten to thirty buyers, in the latter years of the decade. Profit-making assets were bid up to astronomical heights, whether they were publicly or privately held.

Despite such a situation of surplus funds, venture capital investments still favour ideas that can be spun-off into an IPO in the shortest possible time. Only high technology and internet investments have the business plans that can convince investors of this fact in the year 2000. Should these investments begin to show evidence of a setback, or a correction from the early "overshoot" of capital channeled into these sectors, then surplus capital will have even fewer acceptable investments to source. Ultimately, there will exist a very uneven global investment pattern as risk-averse investors will be forced to channel funds into projects that are less and less creditworthy, but this situation will continue to hold as long as the pool of capital continues its expansion. Investment will be characterised as an uneasy truce between low-yielding blue-chip investments and the occasional spurt into uncharted territory. The uncharted territories will be such investments as the "re-emerging markets" and those "dubious" venture capital funds which will claim to return more than twenty-five percent per annum, despite their failings in sourcing strictly high tech and internet investments. The process will continue until there is some crisis as in what happened in 1998, after which investments will be re-channeled back into their safe alternatives with very low yields. Under the new system of globalisation, this pattern can be expected to continue for many years into the future, as long as pressures for low prices together with technological advances continue to exert a revolutionary effect on the G•7 economies.

In our example of the Xvest fund, Scott Ferguson's time will come eventually, perhaps after eighteen months after the latest global market crisis works itself out and yield-hungry investors resume their search for more "exotic" forms of meeting their high yield expectations.

CASINO ECONOMY

Globalisation has created financial "super-cities" in contrast to the declining power of nation states. All of these new power centres such as London, New York, Tokyo, Frankfurt and Paris have been based on a financial service driven economy. The mixture of financial services and increasing technological innovation has created one of the greatest foundations for wealth accumulation. However, the risks for any one of these great financial power centres to lose their leading edge position and fall behind the rest, is always an all too real scenario. Many national legislatures have been forced to tailor their laws in accordance to the wishes of their major financial city centres, accelerating the friction between urban and rural areas.

The move by Germany's politicians over the last decade in promoting Frankfurt as a competitive alternative to both Paris and London, needed a massive overhaul of the German tax code in order to create a competitive environment and one that encouraged restructuring and a greater level of corporate transparency. Not only has the tax code been revised to allow more transparency and greater trading volumes on the Frankfurt Stock Exchange, but a new venture capital market called the "Neuer Markt" is receiving much attention recently.

As nation-states fight to elevate their one-time regional city centres on to the global plane, there exists of real risk to historical financial centres such as London and New York of competitive losses in market share of some form of financial activity. Just as the London based Euro markets were formed under the premise of the U.S. banking system sending capital abroad in order to escape their reserve-ratio requirements, any competitive changes to such regulatory practices could see the outright shift of such a market-making activity to some other geographical part of the world. Although there is a trend developing whereby a common regulatory platform is being adopted generally across all such financial centres in the world, the risks of important financial activity migrating globally has become a real danger to the traditional centres like London and New York.

In many situations where speculative activity became a setback to national monetary and fiscal policies, such as in the early 1990s when the U.K. and Italy were bounced out of the Exchange Rate Mechanism (ERM), many politicians advocated some form of "Tobin Tax" on financial transactions. Not realising that they were now operating within the new system of globalisation, politicians were promoting such taxes on anything from foreign exchange trading to stock market transactions. Under the growing trend towards globalisation, and especially in an area such as financial services, a tax of any type on transactions would instantly drive a valuable segment of market share in such activities to more friendlier parts of the world. Such short-sighted policies were quickly overturned, as leaders of financial centres lobbied the misinformed politicians on potential loss of business. One unique characteristic of competing for financial service and banking activity within any city centre, is that a loss of market share is not quickly replaceable. Often nationalist policies within a region take precedence over following the broader global trend, creating a climate that drives away valuable service activity such as banking and stock broking.

The city of Montreal is a perfect example of how political considerations take precedence over the broader global trend in financial centre development. In the 1950s and the 1960s, Montreal was the undisputed business capital in Canada, until the rise of Québec nationalism drove away a good portion of its business infrastructure to Toronto. At the time, Toronto was merely a regional centre of importance without many prestigious financial service activities, and was certainly anything but a world city centre. However, since the late 1970s, Toronto has registered spectacular gains in the high-end financial service game, becoming a North American city centre of great prominence. A more friendlier climate of taxation, regulation, and social development resulted in an explosion of financial services. Today, it is not uncommon to find over two thousand investment funds that are domiciled in this city, and to find it ranked right up with places like Chicago, San Francisco and Houston in being a major financial services centre in North America. As for Montreal, it has been making a quiet come-back in the global stakes of financial city centres, and has recently concluded a revolutionary agreement with the Nasdaq high technology stock market in New York. It is hoped that the Nasdaq partnership will once again catapult Montreal to a level of prominence among North American financial centres, so that it may recover the lost ground that it relinquished throughout its nationalist period. It has taken the city of Montreal some twenty-five years to re-establish a serious footing in the high stakes of attracting high value-added financial service business, but it still will have some way to go in order to catch up with Toronto.

There is a move recently to merge or create associations for trading platforms across most major financial city centres. Most notably, the London Stock Exchange has moved to align itself with the Frankfurt market, and the electronic based Nasdaq trading system has seen it opportune to branch out into cities such as Montreal and even Tokyo. What this means, is that technological change has made it irrelevant for professionals to be located in any particular city centre state throughout the world, in order to participate in the high value added financial services sector. Day traders working from their farms in Utah or Kansas, can now connect through their telephone lines and take positions directly in stocks and bonds. One global electronic stock market will exert an uncertain effect on established as well as emerging city centre states. It may be the case that infrastructure, or "back-room" activities in banking and broking will eventually be eliminated by technological advancement, whereas the armies of advisors located in places like London and New York will continue to ply their trades in these cities. After all, another very important element to financial city centres, is how attractive an environment they are able to provide the professional class. It may be the case that, as banking and brokerage services become more commoditised and automated, that the primary value-added services will be derived from highly specialised transaction-specific advice. Such specialised professional advice will be bought by other large corporations, and will include such things as research on "exotic" market investments, global merger and acquisition strategies, and the increasingly complex methods of evaluating internet, high tech and new economy stocks and bonds. Not only will financial city centres need to provide the necessary regulatory and tax configurations, but they will also need to address the lifestyle concerns of these types of professionals. In essence, they will need to become great places to live, work and provide cultural activities of interest. For example, it may be very difficult for aspiring venture capital financing city centres, such as Frankfurt, to compete with the location, climate and environment of California's Silicon Valley.

The growing commoditisation and automation of the financial services industry has already exacted a great toll on traditional jobs available to both retail bankers and stock brokers. Companies such as Merrill Lynch that have traditionally employed thousands of individual retail brokers, now must contend with internet-based dealing that is offered for free. Likewise, the heavy investment that was required in brick and mortar branches, is now adequately handled via electronic banking machines located in Wal-Mart stores. Over the past decade, the nature of these activities have been changed full-circle. It is now very difficult to find retail banks that are looking to hire traditional administrative staff for the remaining branches that are still in operation, instead they are now recruiting mainly for customer service representatives and financial product sales staff in call centres.

The more that technology eliminates the mundane activities of companies and further flattens their hierarchical structures, the more will the value-added of financial service operations come from risk-management and strategic advice from highly qualified senior staff that these organisations have opted to keep employed, and who now are coming to define more and more the reputations of these companies. In short, a Merrill Lynch is now obliged to provide a cheap trade, but will ask a premium if the client is looking for some kind of direction and advice in their financial planning requirements. Likewise, a large local company that has traditionally borrowed loans from a commercial bank, will now be willing to pay a premium for advice on global risks, given that it is forced to search for merger and acquisition partners both locally and abroad. Moreover, the Canadian fund manager and investor that has displayed a brilliant track record in selecting the Northern Telecoms and Toronto Dominion Banks of the domestic stock mix, is now willing to offer a premium to advisors having knowledge on stock investments in other parts of the world, in accordance to the recent liberalisations in pension fund laws that have been tabled in the Canadian parliament, and will be forthcoming in most other G•7 countries with the elimination of the "pay-as-you-go" systems.

With fewer restrictions on cross border financial investments and with a proliferation of technology and automation, combined with an era of rising wealth and low-interest money, the actions of traders and speculators have been more visible than ever before. The high priced talent that provides strategy and advice in all major financial city centres, can create not only a trend within the local economy and country, but is now able to cause a global trend across all inter-linked financial city centre states. During the Cold War, closed economies and technological limitations kept an orderly progress and trend intact within the financial centres of each nation-state itself. This trend was subject to the control of monetary, but mainly fiscal policies which served to offset any adverse or negative fluctuations in the local economy's business cycle. However, the current global linkage of markets along with the direct impact that the armies of advisors are able to exert on prices, have created a framework for wild price swings in financial assets such as bonds, but especially stocks and currencies.

The more that the G•7 countries turn their economies in favour of services at the expense of traditional manufacturing, the greater will be the flexibility in support of a free market system that is interlinked globally. What this means is that services offered that are no longer relevant or in demand via the market structure, can more easily be phased out in relation to manufacturing operations which carry large investment costs. The current debate in the UK over inward investments by companies such as Honda, Toyota and Caterpillar, and the ever rising value of sterling affecting export earnings concerns heavy investment in production facilities. Most of these branch plants in the UK employ over five hundred people and they manufacture components for the production chain that are heavily exported to the European continent. An over-valued pound sterling has affected these export earnings of these inward investment subsidiaries since 1997, but only recently have the leaders of these companies begun to complain publicly. Renault CEO Carlos Ghosn, the "le cost-killer" of the entire operation has publicly stated that Renault is looking to divert a substantial amount of investment that was destined to Nissan's Sunderland plant, in favour of the continental countries. Most leaders have called on Prime Minister Tony Blair to announce a definite referendum on the Euro and to set a date for this event to happen. Not only this, but Japanese politicians have also begun to lobby in the interests of all Japanese inward investors in the UK for a change in currency politics.

The point is that although these companies have heavy commitments in the UK, the circumstances make it most difficult to implement an immediate remedy to the situation. Inward investment in the UK is mainly involving heavy industry and heavy investment commitments by these firms, to such an extent that when the market situation calls for a change, it literally takes several years for a shift in production to occur. By contrast, the more that the G•7 countries commit to adopting service economies, the bigger will be the impact on shifting production in accordance to prevailing market conditions. Taken to its extreme level, a shock in one financial centre such as Wall Street, will reverberate in the financial service sectors of all city centre states around the world. The flexibility inherent in financial services, or services of any other sort for that matter, ensures that the economy operates with the utmost level of flexibility and large price swings. The more that the global economy becomes interlinked via a free market mechanism backed by rapid technological and communications innovations, the more will life seem as though we are all a part of a large "casino economy."

THREE INVESTMENT STORIES

In the chapters preceding the present, all themes were basically bound under three fundamental investment categories. Investment that was committed locally or globally by building some form of physical presence that included structures, plant or equipment, to human capital in the form of managers and employees, was termed as being real investment, direct investment or foreign direct investment (FDI), when destined in another country. The largest global players in foreign direct investment included the US with $875 billion committed in 1998; the U.K. with $327 billion in commitments and China with $261 billion. Thereafter followed Germany, France and the Benelux countries as recipients of foreign direct investments.

The nature of foreign direct investment is such that only very large multinational companies are able to manage the risks involved with managing an operation in different countries. More often than not, it is the well known brand names such as Coca-Cola, General Electric and AT&T, that combine with various types of international finance organisations such as the World Bank, Asian Development Bank or European Bank for Reconstruction and Development, to jointly develop permanent operations in countries that do not form the G•7 or OECD groupings. Moreover, the Fortune 500 group of mega corporations are usually far more powerful economically, than are the individual governments that host their investments. Most newly emerging economies in central and eastern Europe, as well as in east and southeast Asia clamour for the attention of the executives of these companies. Very often, very attractive incentives are offered to foreign direct investors to locate their production facilities in these countries. Under a world of increasing transparency in global markets, the techniques and educational value that the Fortune 500 is able to offer is enough to have all emerging market countries deem such investment as highly desirable. Further, my own research indicates that the Fortune 500 are usually not swayed by any tax or fiscal incentives that these countries may offer them, in order to locate in their particular countries. What is usually more important is a history of political stability and democratic institutions that are able to undergo changes with minimal disruption and dislocation. Add to this the benefits of a well educated work force, and most large companies will tell you that these sets of conditions would attract their attention more than the route that offers favourable tax regimes.

The second class of investment has to do with cross border mergers and acquisitions. The pace of cross border acquisitions has never reached the values seen in the latter half of the 1990s. The fight for global market share is a very bloody game, with large mega corporations proceeding to buy their way to "bigness," despite the recent aggressive attempts by the U.S. Federal Trade

Commission to bring many deals under serious scrutiny and investigation. Never before has it been the case that an exotic topic such as cross border acquisitions would make so many headline stories in the mainstream daily press. Most recently, French media and utilities group, Vivendi, has acquired the Canadian drinks, movies and music conglomerate, Seagram. In what to now is the biggest trans-atlantic deal on record, the Europeans will finally exert some influence in the Hollywood film and music studios.

In that respect, cross border mergers and acquisitions have everything to do with managerial control of the assets of the target company in another country. The control over the market share in the foreign country is what has motivated the cross border transaction in the first place. If it was an outright minority position and a straight purchase of shares, then the investment would fall into our next category, which is international or global portfolio allocation.

The typical global fund manager is very careful not to hold more than a minority position in any given company. Institutional fund managers and pension funds are not interested in the day in and day out management of any company. Their minority position, however, entitles them to direct contact with the management of their investment. Periodically, the management of a company is obliged to hold talks with stock market analysts and economists, creating an expectation or forecasting what they believe is the short term direction of its profitability. These formalities are done with the sole interests of all minority investors in mind.

Global portfolio allocations may hold all forms of liquid investments, including Eurobonds denominated in different currencies. It all depends on what the mandate of the investment fund is and how its prospectus or constitution is written up. This form of investment is strictly financial in nature and will have no connection with any form of physical allocation, production or management. If a manager wants to invest in a country, then she will buy the shares of a listed company that may or may not be highly liquid. Alternatively, a fund manager may choose to approach his investment strategy from a sectoral basis, allocating a fixed percentage towards banks, another portion to telecoms companies and the remainder towards heavy industry. The characteristic in common with all strategies and philosophies in this form of investment will be the ease of entry and exit from any individual investment.

These three areas that define investment have been the core foundations by which *The G•7 Report Project* was executed and extended throughout the 1990s; this new era of globalisation. They were all inter-connected by the emergence of an ultra-efficient global financial marketplace, that was linked by the massive volumes evident on the world's currency markets. Currency markets were the link between various legal jurisdictions, and they connected both public and private entities in commercial activities in one form or another.

Furthermore, international commerce was also connected by the physical existence of trade relationships. The flipside to an international financial transaction was usually the underlying physical presence of a trade or direct investment action. These actions were usually not as immediate as their financial counterparts, and were therefore lagged for a period of a year or more.

Stock markets have also seen major changes that have upset their usual clubby activity within national jurisdictions, just as international barriers to equity investing have collapsed. Soon there will be just one global market, interconnected via some form of internet and operated as a global Nasdaq market. The fact that the New York Nasdaq market has become a global icon, is testimony to the demand for innovation in execution. What is next could very well be some form of electronic interconnection among all computer screens and terminals around the world as the only remaining stock exchange.

In this respect, there has become one enormous equity market or "equity pool" to be more accurate, where companies wishing to raise capital may decide against listing in their home markets, and instead go straight to those markets that are best able to suit their requirements. Further, in the new era of one global stock market, companies have also opted to proceed with multiple listings that satisfy the demands of institutional investors in more than one financial city centre. More than ever before, there is one global stock market that links up equity buyers and sellers.

Diverting briefly from our primary manuscript; the three areas of investment that make up the broader definition of investment, are joined by venture capital investing. Venture capital has come to play a fairly prominent role in the latter half of the 1990s, particularly in the U.S. high technology sector. Venture capital is a class of investment that is unique, and which has very little to do with our three standard classifications of foreign direct investment, cross border mergers and acquisitions and global portfolio allocations. Each of these have more to do with a much later stage of corporate development, whereas venture capital is a commitment or backing of a marketable idea. It is risk capital in its purest form, and a category in which *The G•7 Report Project* was eager to participate in, solely from the angle that there was too much money in the 1990s chasing too few investment opportunities, and the large corporations were perfectly content to pursue downsizing via aggressive acquisitions of market share. With such a huge pool of global investment capital available, the development of venture capital was a natural event and one that deserved full attention. The financial development of marketable ideas was an activity that was unique in the era of globalisation, and which came to define the notable developments of the latter half of the 1990s.

MYSTERY CAPITAL

Albert Friedberg was considered by many to be the Canadian version of George Soros. In May of 2000, he wrote an open letter to his clients admitting that the rules of the currency investment game have changed, and that the once spectacular returns which all were accustomed to were now much more difficult to attain. Almost simultaneously, George Soros in New York moved to downsize his hedge fund program by inviting all investors to redeem their investments, if they still thought that average returns of thirty percent per annum or more were achievable. In his latter years, Soros was reported as opting to spend more time giving away his accumulated personal savings to good causes in central and eastern Europe, while he was willing to live with rates of return that were around the ten to fifteen percent benchmark.

The nature of the market for currency investing has changed to such an extent, that two of the most respected speculators in the business decided to publicly announce, that even they were having difficulty in the markets. The Friedberg letter draws references to these fast changing currency markets: "...Currency rates are largely determined by the capital flows of international, and mainly institutional, investors. In the old days- that's to say, prior to 1997- international and institutional investors were happy with incremental advantages in risk-free securities." He goes on to give a hypothetical example: "If a treasurer at Dresdner Bank could earn 50 basis points more in U.S. t-bills than he could in the German equivalent, and he believed that the dollar would not fall by more than his 50 basis point advantage, boom: he sold marks, bought dollars, and the dollar went up against the mark. In other words, if you could predict changes in interest rates in different countries, you had a leg up on predicting currency rates."

Traditionally, the currency markets were a link as well as a signal as to how a particular country was performing in its traded sectors. If there was a trade surplus as in the case of the Japanese auto trade in the 1980s, then the market value of the yen would increase. Conversely, if there was a trade deficit then a currency would depreciate on the condition that floating exchange rates were in operation. If a country was operating under a fixed exchange rate regime, then a trade deficit would traditionally be paid by a transfer of gold reserves, or in the case of the U.S. and Japan; the Japanese would end up accepting to buy U.S. treasury bills. As the Friedberg letter argues: "...Throughout the 1980s treasurers of international financial institutions were concerned with trade balances. Then he who could predict trade balances had a leg up on predicting currency rates. . ..Prior to 1972 nearly all international currency transactions were for the purpose of settling commercial trade contracts. Today 99 percent of transactions relate to investment flows. The transition from trade to investment happened during the 1980s."

Also, during the early years of capital liberalisation within the G•7 countries, it was the short term real rate of return differentials among risk-free bonds, that determined how investment flows worked. The dynamic during the Cold War years was fairly straight forward, if a country moved to re-inflate without the support of other countries in co-ordinating such a re-inflation, as was the case of France and the early Mitterrand years in the early 1980s, then the franc would fall on foreign exchange markets since the real interest rate differential would not change.

By contrast, when Bundesbank President Helmut Schlesinger moved to raise the lombard and discount rates in Germany after the re-unification boom had occurred, the Deutsche mark hit record levels against the dollar. The increase in short term rates was engineered during a period of non-monetary inflation with no intentions by the German central bank to engage in an inflationary increase. With already low inflation prior to re-unification, the rise in short term rates was considered to be the equivalent of an insurance policy against demand-generated inflation that may have occurred as a result of the re-unification. These increases in the early 1990s inspired a massive inflow into Deutsche mark-denominated risk-free investments, and an equivalent massive outflow from U.S. dollar denominated assets. For currency speculators and traders, this period was one of the most easiest to predict, hence making spectacular gains in managing currency-oriented funds. If there was ever a currency event where *The G•7 Report's* forecasts were right on the money, this was it. To have been bullish on the Deutsche mark throughout the early years of the 1990s, meant that long position takers fully understood the glorious history of the Bundesbank.

In the case of the Mitterrand re-inflation, it was a well-known fact that the Banque de France, the central bank, had no history of independence from its political masters. Consequently, a move to simply print more money for social spending and demand-management of the economy would merely devalue the external value of the franc, and would leave the real rate of interest exactly where it was prior to the experiment. In the final result, France may have gained a brief uptick in its trade surplus due to the lower franc, but this would have been temporary and would have been closed-off, once the re-inflation began to increase the prices on all domestically-produced goods that would have been exported.

The re-unification induced inflation was different, not only from the perspective that the German central bank had a glorious independent history, but also since re-unification was a non-monetary event which happened on the real side of the economy. In essence, it was a "structural" change in the geography of the country that may have produced an increase in prices, should precautionary measures by the Bundesbank have not materialised by an increase in short term real interest rates and a rising Deutsche mark.

By the 1980s, financial innovations combined with technological and communications inventions, helped create the foundation for global portfolio investing. As international capital markets began to open up and laws were passed in Europe to encourage full capital mobility prior to the formal adoption of the single European currency, the importance of trade flows in determining the value of currencies began to diminish. In fact, one of the factors that caused an abrupt ending to the Cold War era was the rising mobility of global capital flows, which effectively worked to break down financial barriers and encouraged growth in international trade and commerce outside of the G•7 countries. So fast was the substitution away from trade-driven currency values, to mobile capital flow-driven global currency markets, that many fund managers were caught off guard.

The fall of the Berlin Wall signalled that the era of globalisation would elevate the prominence of global portfolio investments even further. As the 1990s progressed, it was no longer portfolio investments in risk-free bonds that determined currency parities between countries, but now an equity portion was beginning to assume a large degree of prominence. Albert Friedberg writes: "In 1997 the game started to change. Then, for the first time, the siren of the stock market called these treasurers too..." The mighty "blue-chip" corporation which was getting larger and larger by engaging in record merger and acquisition activity throughout the 1990s, was now viewed as a perfect substitute by many portfolio managers. Realising that these organisations were larger than the tax base of many countries that they operated in, their power became a very attractive positioning point in many global portfolios.

Furthermore, currency values were also affected by an entirely new global capital flow, once again. As mentioned above, the record breaking merger and acquisition activity in the G•7, created a global market for corporate control, as the large Fortune 500 companies rushed to consolidate their market shares under this new era of a heightened state of competition. Not only did the currency risk arbitrageur have to take into account the direction of global portfolio flows in stocks and bonds, but they now also needed to contend with cross border merger and acquisition transactions, for both public as well as privately-owned companies.

If trying to predict the direction of risk-free rates of return was too much, then the newer paradigms of which stock trends either attracted or dislodged capital, became even more difficult to ascertain. The most difficult trends to recognise are cross border mergers and acquisitions, but these have been the life blood of the US dollar throughout the period between 1998 to 2000. Never before has the flow of capital been so skewed in America's favour, when looking at the outflows originating in the European Union. European companies have assumed a level of aggressiveness never before evident, as they move to grab market shares in the U.S. by buying some of the largest corporate groups known. This activity has been so startlingly apparent, that both mergers and acquisitions and foreign direct investments destined to the U.S. from Europe, have gone as far as eclipsing the importance of pure global portfolio allocations over the past two years.

Traditionalists and economists know that something is not right, when the European Central Bank moves to raise its short term interest rates by one percentage point and no noticeable effect occurs to the Euro in relation to the dollar or the yen. Traditional economic relationships between rates of return and values have undergone somewhat of a transformation recently, as capital flows are now motivated by a number of factors, including the traditional commercial trade flows which were so vitally important just a decade ago.

THE U.S. AND THE DOLLAR

One very important area that came to define *The G•7 Report* newsmagazine was my regular review, analysis and forecast of the major currencies that made up the G•7 countries. What I noticed most when following both short and longer term trends, was how often pure analysis based on sole economic and financial factors was often groundless in trying to understand short-term outcomes. The global currency market is far more liquid, and exceeds by far the aggregate transaction volumes on all of the major global stock exchanges grouped together. As discussed in the previous chapter, global capital flows have constantly evolved and changed over the past three decades, to the extent that the current eclectic mix of factors that move this market are more than ever, difficult to judge. Not only are there portfolio decision factors based on traditional rates of return arguments, behind massive capital movements internationally, but now equally important are factors such as foreign direct investments, as well as the more abstract cross border merger and acquisitions component, in determining the direction of the major currencies. The direction of these investment factors are individually difficult to determine, not to mention the net aggregate effects when all are taken into consideration together, along with their ultimate effects on currencies and major blue chip stocks.

Furthermore, academic economists have raised their hands up in a gesture of surrender, claiming that the currency market behaves as though it is engaged in a constant "random walk" pattern. For those unfamiliar with the random walk theory, it stipulates that forecasting is impossible for variables which behave in such a pattern historically. An advocate of the random walk approach would predict that a currency's value would be about the same as it is at this very moment in relation to another major currency or benchmark. For instance, if I were an advocate of the random walk theory, and someone asked me to forecast where the U.S. dollar would be in relation to the yen, given that it is trading at ¥105 to one U.S. dollar at this moment; I would simply respond by saying: "I forecast that the U.S. dollar would buy ¥105 yen." Personally, I have no problem with this theory if its time frame is instantaneous or within several minutes or the span of one trading day. However, when one looks at a chart over several years to several decades at the dollar/yen parity, there exists an undeniable longer term trend which is susceptible to forecasts over the medium and longer term. This has been the motivation behind my periodic "currency reports," by combining cold economic theoretical reasoning with a greater amount of practical good sense and history.

The goal has always been to forecast currency values that had a chance of being better than fifty percent right. In retrospect, there were certain times when this approach performed extremely well, while also some periods where its record was less than acceptable. I called the Deutsche mark and U.S. dollar parity the best, along with the Italian lira and the Canadian dollar, while my views on the yen/U.S. dollar relationship were the weakest. The highlight of the currency reports came early in the 1990s, when pressure had built up in the European Exchange Rate Mechanism over Germany's re-unification plans. As the Bundesbank pursued a uni-dimensional monetary policy designed to address the escalating concerns over inflation, at the expense of its shared obligations among its European partners, I felt that something more dramatic had to occur even though George Soros had already dramatically broke the pound sterling. What resulted was a devaluation in the Italian lira and the ensuing widening of the 2.25 percent fluctuation bands to fifteen percent on either side, hence allowing the French franc a face-saving adjustment which really turned out to be a massive devaluation, except that no European officials were allowed to use this term by name. *The G•7 Report* early on forecasted that a devaluation was imminent, even before the move by Soros on sterling had occurred. It was illogical to have a regime of fixed exchange rates, and full capital mobility within the Euro zone along with a chronic lack of fundamental convergence between member states.

The U.S. dollar was a story of strict trade flow adjustments in the 1980s, and short term interest rate differentials in the early 1990s relative to the Deutsche mark and the currencies that made up the Exchange Rate Mechanism. By contrast, the dollar/yen parity in the early 1990s was strictly a relationship that was governed by trade rhetoric. In a way it was an extension of the situation that had existed during the Reagan administration in the 1980s, where the G•7 Plaza and Louvre accords were used to re-align the major exchange rates in accordance to the emerging trade realities at the time. Consequently, the massive Japanese trade surplus began in the mid 1980s, as demand for smaller automotive products by the American public was not being met by the "big 3" producers in Detroit. This "trade surplus politics" as it became called, went as long as the mid 1990s, well after the Cold War era was over and the new globalisation system was in full swing.

During the term of the Reagan administration, the U.S. for the first time ever was reduced to accepting its status as being a debtor country, as Treasury Secretary James Baker moved to raise the agenda of trade politics with Japan to such an extent that a sudden realignment took place in their respective currencies. Policy was really no different under the four year tenure of the Bush administration from 1988 to 1992. Treasury Secretary Nicholas Brady was even more forceful in communicating with the Japanese over the burgeoning trade imbalances with the U.S. As the recession of 1990 began to take hold of the U.S. economy, the "Big 3" auto producers were more aggressive than ever before in moving to protect their domestic market shares. A rising Japanese trade surplus during this period, was painted as an attack on U.S. jobs, despite the fact that a program of massive direct investment was beginning to take hold by all of the Japanese automotive producers, as they moved to aggressively expand production in the local U.S. market.

What was unique during this time, is that the movement of the yen became inextricably linked to trade rhetoric. When the Japanese trade surplus vis-à-vis the U.S. went up, and U.S. officials became vocal about it, the value of the yen went up. Even when U.S. officials did not say a word to the media, and there was evidence of a rising trade surplus, traders pushed up the value of the yen. Never before was there a currency relationship quite like this. It was as if the U.S. was using the Japanese yen as a tool of its foreign trade policy, simply by calling in the major media groups based in Washington D.C. or in New York and voicing their discontent over the imbalances. This certainly was not something that was normal in any other currency relationship in recent history. Consequently, many traders, fund managers and company treasurers who were unable to discern this trend, missed the mark in their dollar/yen hedging strategies. One had to be an astute political analyst, that was able to foresee a heightened state of friction in the Japanese and U.S. trading relationship, in order to make a good judgement and forecast in this market during the time period between 1985 and 1995.

When evidence surfaced that Japan was in the midst of its deepest economic downturn in history, and the Bank of Japan moved to its "zero overnight interest rate" policy in the latter half of the 1990s, the U.S. toned down its trade rhetoric. The domestic auto industry was once again feeling good, since it was producing an aggregate amount of vehicles well above its historic average of fourteen million units per annum, and both profits and share prices were breaking records. Also, the overall climate in the U.S. was euphoric, as housing starts were never better, and consumer confidence was buoyed by the rising wealth effect created in the stock markets. At the height of the trade rhetoric period, the yen peaked at ¥79 to one dollar, while a few years later when evidence surfaced that the "bubble economy" of the late 1980s still did not hit bottom, and the once mighty Japanese banks were on the verge of bankruptcy, the yen made an abrupt reversal and slid as low as ¥150 to the dollar. The savvy investor who held yen and bought the dollar at its low; then again selling the dollar when it peaked relative to the yen, would have made a spectacular gain in excess of two hundred percent during this time of crisis-induced fluctuation.

The latter half of the 1990s was a period when severe imbalances began to surface in the domestic Japanese economy. Banks never really climbed out of their problems after being left with a slew of non-performing property loans from the "bubble years" of the late 1980s, and one major automotive manufacturer, Nissan, was actually bought up by Renault of France. The chronic underperformance in Japan's retail sector, also created concern since consumer spending was the engine behind two-thirds of all income that was generated in the economy. The U.S. continued to observe trade developments from the sidelines, without actively intervening verbally if evidence surfaced that the surplus was on the way up again. It was more concerned about the persistent depression in the local economy of Japan, and the fact that the collapse of the "bubble years" still have not worked themselves out of the economic system by now. The collapse of the Cold War hit all members of the G•7, and the rise of globalisation was accepted in varying degrees. It could be said that Japan found it the most difficult to adjust to the new openness that is demanded among major financial centres such as Tokyo.

For one, financial transparency and corporate governance were concepts very foreign to the traditional culture and norms of doing business within Japan. For years, the major U.S. auto producers criticised the system better known as "keiretsu" among Japan's corporate groupings. The cross-shareholdings within corporate cluster companies served to protect the local market from foreign intruders. It was enormously difficult for even powerful companies such as Ford Motor to penetrate the Japanese marketplace with their line of vehicles.

This system was fine during the closed economies of the Cold War, but was not viable under the new high tech and competitive economic system. As the 1980s drew to a close, the wild speculative binges in commercial property were over, but many advanced G•7 countries dealt quickly with the malaise by allowing both property developers, as well as their bankers to go into bankruptcy. In the U.S., the Resolution Trust Corporation set up during the Reagan and Bush administrations, served to liquidate insolvent savings and loans institutions, which were caught in the midst of the spectacular melt-down.

Likewise, in Canada and in the U.K., the collapse of the property booms brought many years of despair and recession. In the Canadian case, Toronto was hit very badly, as the large banks moved quickly to seize as collateral the insolvent properties making up most of its downtown core. Only in the latter half of the 1990s, did the Toronto market begin to recover from the impact felt during the crisis years of the early 1990s. The experience in the U.K., and more specifically the city of London, was equally as harsh, but the recovery began a few years earlier when compared to the Canadian case. The spectacular collapse of the Canary Wharf project in London's Docklands which was a symbol of the ending of the era of property speculation in the late 1980s, was turned into a profitable project in the latter half of the 1990s. By contrast, the property sector in Japan is still depressed with no end to the malaise. Whenever signs emerge of a turnaround, yet another bank or financial institution collapses based on massive loans outstanding and uncollectible from a property developer.

Only recently, did Japan allow foreign private equity funds to rummage through its non-performing assets, in the hopes that they could come up with a plan that would be viable, and which would save the jobs that were about to disappear. Throughout this severe adjustment period, the Bank of Japan pursued what became known as the "zero overnight rate" policy. Meaning that it was prepared to lend very short term funds at no cost to bank borrowers. What was unique about this policy is that the yen value did not fluctuate erratically, but found an equilibrium level relative to the dollar somewhere within the trading band of ¥100 to ¥110. Without a doubt, if it were any other central bank that tried to pursue such a "free money" policy, their respective currencies would be hammered in the global currency markets. Why did the yen not behave in a like manner? No one can really tell for sure, but a lot has to do with the fact that the yen is influenced far more by politics and sentiment, than by pure market factors.

Therefore, it is far easier to forecast the dollar/Euro parity than it is the dollar/yen. An economic purist will be pleased to see that the dollar/Euro parity behaves in accordance to market-driven principles of inflationary expectations, interest rates and overall business conditions and economic growth prospects for the countries in question. The same purist will cringe, and will dislike any discussion or mention of the dollar/yen outlook. It remains a wonder to me, even to this day, why many treasurers and global fund managers attempt to take some sort of long or short position on the dollar/yen parity. One must not only be brave, but possess some kind of extraordinary ability in order to be a player in this speculative game.

As for the case of the U.S. dollar, the political bias throughout the 1980s favoured a devaluation based purely on the deteriorating balance of trade accounts. The massive demand-led expansion engineered by the administration of Ronald Reagan, resulted in a global imbalance, as U.S. consumers sucked in record luxury imports, expanding the balance of trade deficit. In a way, the U.S. was in uncharted waters throughout this period, as never before in the 1960s and 1970s, was it in such a position as a "debtor country." If the Reagan administration had any kind of policy towards the dollar, it was either to let it follow a "monetarist" prescription and allow it to be determined in the global currency markets, or to push through a devaluation in order to re-balance the trade accounts with countries such as Japan, Germany and Italy.

The Paul Volcker era Federal Reserve, which ran from 1980 to 1987, brought with it a strong dollar policy, if only by default. The move to address the inflationary problems of the 1970s, resulted in record levels of interest rates in the early 1980s, as the federal funds rate hit as high as eighteen percent, and continued to persistently hover above twelve percent until well into the middle of the decade. During these years, the dollar shot into an area of new strength, as it was traded from a position of strength. Meanwhile, the trade balance was deteriorating, as consumers moved to buy the much desired and ultra-cheap Japanese automotive imports. When Alan Greenspan was appointed as the Chairman of the Federal Reserve in 1987 from his private sector consulting practice, the G•7 had already decided that a co-ordinated intervention in the currency markets was much to be desired. Greenspan, almost simultaneously, engineered a soft-landing in the economy when the Dow Jones industrial average crashed in 1987, by immediately pushing U.S. rates lower in order to offset the loss of confidence created by this financial meltdown. In essence, the co-ordinated devaluation in the U.S. dollar accomplished by general agreement among the G•7 countries, in what became known as the Plaza accords, was confirmed by the move of official interest rates downwards in order to address the stock market crisis head on. The lower dollar value, needed a lower official rate of interest by the Fed in order to achieve consistency in its devalued state. This was successfully accomplished throughout the latter half of the 1980s.

As the Cold War ended and an entirely new and different period began, the U.S. as well as Canada and the U.K., were quick to re-adjust through some far reaching economic re-structuring. They were in an entirely different cycle, when German re-unification prompted the Bundesbank in Germany to begin a series of rate increases, to offset the inflationary impact that a misjudged and overvalued conversion rate for eastern marks into the Deutsche mark brought about. For that matter, most European continental countries did not experience the severity of the recession in the early 1990s, and the Bush administration did absolutely nothing within the realm of currency politics in order to change the general direction of the dollar, which was downwards. The period from 1991 to 1994 could be considered to be the era of the Deutsche mark. As short term rate differentials between German and U.S. assets drove the mark higher. In fact, the mark was so strong under the tenure of the then President of the Bundesbank, Helmut Schlesinger, that crisis ensued within the region of Europe. France, Italy as well as Sweden, felt unbearable strain in the currency parities as the Bundesbank acted unilaterally to quell the rising inflation that resulted from the re-unification of the two Germanies.

By the time the Clinton administration was elected, ousting the unpopular Bush, a new political agenda was in the air for the U.S. dollar. The benign neglect, combined with economic underperformance, which became a hallmark of the Bush era, quickly was transformed into a proactive policy which favoured a stronger dollar. On many occasions, the then Secretary of the Treasury Lloyd Bentsen, was always quick to point out that the administration favoured a strong dollar. The Clinton administration moved to encourage massive capital inflows into the U.S., hence exploiting the new era of global capital mobility; the rise of international mergers and acquisitions and the creation of newly emerging markets. By doing very little in the area of policy, and by allowing the market to freely determine where capital was to flow, the Clinton administration, rightly or wrongly, was credited as having unleashed a brave new era and dynamism in the domestic U.S. economy.

The promotion of the internet and various other forms of technological innovation was its crowning achievement. The U.S. economy gained an inertia of its own, laying the foundations for a structural shift upwards in stock prices, hence creating a wealth effect that was unparalleled in the recent past. This dynamism by itself attracted praise and attention, as it pulled investors in Europe and Asia towards its new and booming economy. As the U.S. restructured in the 1990s, it was as much as three years ahead of its European counterparts. The dynamism that drew interest and capital inflows, gave the dollar a solid foundation and reason for further appreciation. In the end, even Fed Chairman Alan Greenspan, admitted that the economy has turned a new and more productive chapter in recent economic history.

THE EURO

European countries were frantically trying to achieve a level of convergence in the 1990s. The Maastricht Treaty stipulated that debts must be below sixty percent to GDP, and that deficits could not exceed three percent of GDP, in order for member states to be admitted into the new single currency of Europe. What were countries such as Italy and Belgium to do, since their debts exceeded one hundred and twenty percent of GDP in any given year? Such questions just scratched the surface of the problems plaguing the single currency project right from the start. The trick was to co-ordinate, by January of 1999, the disposal of each country's national currency at the wholesale level, since actual Euros in circulation would not begin until 2002. The challenge facing most European countries in the early 1990s, when the Maastricht Treaty was drafted and implemented, was to carry through with their promises until the very end. Not an easy task, given that many countries in Europe had a history of political crises and market based institutions were not so developed, yet the Maastricht Treaty was in itself, very much a market-driven document that demanded a strict market solution to Europe's financial challenges.

The problem facing European companies, was that the capital markets in individual countries were not very well developed; were too shallow and were more or less illiquid. In this respect, the Euro was a grand idea, since what European users of capital really needed were an efficient market that had a high degree of liquidity. Logically, if only all of the highly fragmented local markets could come together as one, capital and a high level of liquidity would be a real benefit for the growth of GDP. In other words, if companies could have more access to capital and less reliance on the banking establishments in Europe, efficiency and growth would go hand-in-hand.

The Euro was only introduced at the very tail end of the decade of globalisation. Most of Europe's policy framework in this era was solely oriented in achieving this single goal. The sacrifices in which Italy and Belgium had to make in order to qualify, are still being felt by their industrial sectors. Clearly, Germany was the leader throughout this decade, and the Deutsche mark was the benchmark under which all of the European member states tied their currencies to. The Bundesbank was the central bank that was independent, and brought forth a textbook example in how monetary policy should be conducted. Most other continental European countries did not have such a tradition of independence, as their central banks were tied to their respective treasuries, hence susceptible to political interference and meddling.

The plan early on was to somehow buy credibility from the Bundesbank by pegging the French franc and Italian lira to the Deutsche mark. Only then would the Euro zone move in one direction, hence offering a better chance of actually converging all of its economies together in one direction. This approach was only credible as long as investors armed with global capital mobility, perceived those countries that opted to peg their currencies to the mark, as having the ability to keep pace, and to restructure in a more productive way. The new system of globalisation came, when only Germany was truly prepared in terms of having an existing institutional infrastructure, that would be in a position to serve the rising private institutional investors in Europe. At a minimum, an independent central bank was required in order to be credible from a policy perspective in this brave new era.

In the 1970s, prior to any blueprint or order in European currency markets, it was quite easy to make money speculating on the direction of either the franc, lira or the mark. All what was needed was some intuition over the balance of trade in relation to the anchor, which was the German mark. By the time German Chancellor Helmut Schmidt and French President Valéry Giscard d'Estaing got around to proposing the European Monetary System in 1979, currency speculators had already had their day. In the early 1980s, betting against the basket of European currencies in light of the record rise in short term rates in the U.S., as instigated by the then Chairman of the Federal Reserve, Paul Volcker, would have been the optimal scenario as the European Monetary System was still in its infancy. Also, throughout the 1980s, individual European countries began to join the European currency framework one-by-one. The accession of Italy and the U.K., was later joined by Spain and Portugal, as European countries felt an urgency to halt the destructive currency fluctuations within their trading zone.

Once again in the late 1980s, it was opportune to be long on the Deutsche mark in relation to the dollar. When the G•7 negotiated Plaza Accords called for a co-ordinated devaluation in the dollar and revaluation of European currencies, it was once again trade balances that were at the centre of the event. The late 1980s, just prior to the ending of the Cold War, seemed to be the glory years for European monetary and currency policy initiatives. The European Monetary System was working well, as was the Exchange Rate Mechanism which governed the allowable 2.25 percent fluctuation of all member countries' currencies. Also, it was still the era of trade balance-driven fluctuations, where capital flows were not as yet unleashed.

The ensuing fall of the Berlin Wall, and the new era of globalisation together with fast and furious international capital flows proved a challenge for the entire single currency project. It was very difficult to maintain a pegged parity in light of something close to perfect capital mobility. In 1992, the pound sterling and the Italian lira uncoupled from the pegged European Exchange Rate Mechanism, and fell to historic lows in relation to the dollar. However, the Deutsche mark pursued its own independent path during these years, and strengthened in relation to the dollar. The single currency project was near collapse, when in the summer of 1993, the French franc could no longer keep up with the high rates of interest in Germany after re-unification, and was effectively devalued by fifteen percent. Once again, the Euro zone of currencies seemed to be all over the place, without the much needed guidance of targets that the Exchange Rate Mechanism provided. Even though the Deutsche mark on its own provided gains to those that had a long position on it, most other European currencies lost value in relation to the dollar, despite dollar weakness.

After several years of "cooling off" the single currency project once again began to pick up momentum, as Germany was now in recession herself, and her arch rival, France was making productivity gains within the Euro zone. The improvement in French competitiveness during the mid 1990s, justified many in saying that France was now ahead of Germany in its efforts to restructure within the Euro zone, and join the global economy as it was evolving. Its corporate activity was far more international than was Germany's, and moves to quietly reform its civil service and institutions did not go unnoticed. Moreover, Italy and Belgium moved to substantially reduce their public debts, so as to meet the convergence criteria of the Maastricht Treaty for single currency participation. This was accomplished by a combination of great sacrifice in raising a multitude of taxes, as well as a few accounting "tricks." By 1997, enough momentum was created and crises of the past were fading memories, as Europe was moving towards the launch of the single currency. By this time, trading opportunities with the dollar have become less than profitable, as the wide swings seen in the 1980s trade-induced adjustments, and the early 1990s crises with the Deutsche mark, paled in comparison with the shorter swing patterns and relative calm in the latter part of the decade.

Severe fluctuations only occurred after the introduction of the Euro, and in relation to non-participating currencies such as the U.S. dollar and the pound sterling. On January 1, 1999, European member states moved to irrevocably lock their currency parities in the following manner: One Euro was valued at 1.96 Deutsche marks; 13.76 Austrian Schillings; 40.34 Belgian francs; 2.20 Dutch Guilders; 5.95 Finnish Markka, 6.56 French francs; 0.79 Irish Punts; 1,936.27 Italian lira; 40.34 Luxembourg francs; 200.48 Portuguese Escudos and 166.39 Spanish Pesetas. The Euro itself made its debut around $1.18, but quickly adjusted downwards throughout 1999. Another one of our projections which was accurate, was the call made on the direction of the Euro/dollar parity. *The G•7 Report* was a lone voice in forecasting a weaker Euro, after most economists, analysts and commentators predicted that the new currency would immediately gain acceptance along with strength in global currency markets. Our argument was more abstract, since the newly-formed Euro was only a factor in major institutional and wholesale capital markets; an emerging bond market in Europe denominated in one currency was one of the most dramatic developments that could have occurred after its launch. I argued that the only immediate players in Euros would be the ultra "blue-chip" companies and institutions, testing out the deepening of the European capital markets. They would then move to issue bonds denominated in the new Euro, but would shift this capital that was raised out of the Euro zone and back to either Japan or the U.S. We should keep in mind that U.S. companies were the most aggressive in using the bond markets, while European companies traditionally used bank credits. Therefore, the Euro market was very much affected initially by this differing cultural approach in corporate finance. U.S. companies and various international government institutions would be the real drivers of the value of the Euro in the initial years.

As it happened, the Euro kept sinking on the global currency markets, breaching the $0.86 cents level; a far cry from its initial launch value of $1.18. What had occurred was a re-positioning of corporate balance sheets to take account of the new currency in the international marketplace. What was an impossibility when French francs, Portuguese Escudos and Austrian Schillings were still around, quickly developed as the capital market in Europe expanded to the level of the U.S. bond market in one short year. However, the Euro paid for this expansion in the international markets, as those that aggressively raised capital repatriated a large portion of these funds back into U.S. dollars or Japanese yen. Also, the low rate of interest payable on Euro liabilities was a very attractive incentive to all corporate treasurers in managing their funding needs. This is the main reason why the Euro is performing badly in the global currency markets, and is expected to continue until rates go up to the levels seen in U.S. markets, or corporate treasury activities come to an acceptable balance between the major currencies in the world. The few that forecast the fall in the Euro, would have made spectacular gains in their short hedging activities in relation to the yen and the dollar.

In retrospect, the European Central Bank was right in holding off any increases in short term rates in order to help the ailing Euro, since most of the adjustment was "structural" in nature, and any move to support it in global currency markets would have ultimately caused more harm than good. At this moment, it seems as though the development of the European wholesale capital markets has been nearly completed, and the Euro has found its equilibrium trading range between $0.85 and $1.00. At one point, the old Deutsche mark equivalent to the U.S. dollar surpassed Dm. 2.30, a level not seen since the 1980s. Once this structural shift in the European wholesale capital markets plays itself out, trading conditions will never really recover to a pattern of normality. We should remember that European corporations are now some of the most aggressive acquirors of U.S. based companies, and foreign direct investment on behalf of European corporates is at a record level in the U.S. market. Much of this direct investment activity is driven by the high tech sector, and was four times larger in 1999 than in 1997. The old differences in short term rates will never be able to exert the effects that they had in the early 1990s. This time and era is over when looking at the developments in the tail end of the decade, and the big question is whether these old traditional relationships will ever again be good predictors of the dollar/euro parity in the global currency markets. My personal opinion is that short term rate spreads will have marginal impacts on this trading relationship. The overall effect that will move the dollar/euro will be more accurately divided between the rate spread theory; the newly-developing cross-border merger and acquisition activity; the foreign direct investment flows and the powerful attraction of global stock market investing. Of these three, I would say that the stock market trends and the marginal short term rate spreads will most likely rank ahead of the other two in forecasting the dollar/euro. I rank cross-border mergers and acquisitions lower, since the current record activity is unlikely to continue at its present pace, given that the anti-trust units in the form of the Federal Trade Commission (FTC) in Washington D.C. and its counterparts in Brussels, the Competition Directorate under Mario Monti, have begun to aggressively assert their opposition to several recent blockbuster mega-deals.

How not to Trade the Yen

As was discussed in previous chapters, the Japanese yen is one of the hardest currencies to understand from the perspective of straight economic analysis. Its behaviour does not easily lend itself to this form of analysis, and those currency fund managers that constantly insist on taking out long or short positions in relation to the dollar or the yen, end up losing big. Such a manager would do much better in approaching Japan and the yen from an entirely different discipline and by trying to understand a combination of prevailing market sentiment, history, politics and sociology. My own bias is to leave any yen based exposures to a minimum, but this is easier said than done in an era when the Japanese government bond market is becoming the world's largest, overtaking the U.S. treasury bill issuance program.

Institutional investors have always relied on a plentiful float of U.S. treasuries in order to top-up their risk-free components of their portfolios. Both the U.S.

treasury and the U.K. gilt float has been falling over the past two years, in light of the rapidly changing budgetary positions of these countries. While it is in the best interest of taxpayers to be subjected to surplus positions in a country's fiscal position, the less is the need for issuing bonds as a form of borrowing, which releases less risk-free investment alternatives for investors and savers to hold. What has been happening in the past several years that is less obvious, is that the U.S. bond markets are slowly being absorbed by an ever expanding Japanese risk-free issue market. The less bonds that are floated by the U.S. Treasury to investors, since there is less of a need to finance a budget deficit, the more will these investors search for a substitute in the international markets. The yen denominated float of expanding risk-free bonds will come to play a vital role in plugging the gap that the U.S. Treasury will leave over the upcoming decade.

Should Japanese risk-free bonds replace U.S. treasuries in institutional portfolios, what will the implications be for the yen in the international markets? For one, the money raised will be used to sterilise the bankrupt Japanese corporate system, as well as create more make-work infrastructure spending projects. In addition, since these bonds are denominated in yen, investors will access the global currency markets and exchange dollars and euros for yen, hence driving up the value of the Japanese currency, despite the fact that yields are just marginally higher than zero. For investors to demand these bonds, they must feel comfortable about the currency risks associated with the yen. If they believe that there is a low level of risk in the yen going an adverse way, then they will eagerly buy the new issues. Also, should the redemption of U.S. treasuries and U.K. gilts be accelerated, as tax revenues continue to outpace expenditures, then the supply of traditional bonds will go down more than expected, leaving no alternative but to purchase the Japanese paper. These developments are also powerful evidence in support of the yen over the year 2000, despite the continuation of the "zero overnight interest rate" policy practised by the Bank of Japan. In other words, a very compelling argument can be made in favour of this global shift theory, where a shrinking supply of traditional Treasury bills and bonds, is being replaced by Japanese government issued bonds in the portfolios of major institutional investors. The constant demand for this class of risk-free asset will ensure that the yen will be supported in the global currency markets, despite the low rate of return on yen-denominated assets. Therefore, globalisation is providing a very compelling argument in support of the Japanese currency, just when all of the traditional economic and financial factors seem to have broken down.

The yen is the most politicised currency in the world today. From the 1980s trade wars in the automotive sector, the U.S. acted together with its G•7 counterparts in striking a politically appropriate balance among exchange rates. The

"Plaza Accords" in 1985 negotiated in New York, set about to re-align both the Japanese yen as well as the Deutsche mark. However, the target was clearly the yen, since the "big 3" U.S. auto producers were caught in a desperate situation that not only rejected their product based on gasoline consumption efficiency standards, but they were also caught with some very poor product on offer.

The trade-driven currency policy that came to define the G•7 co-ordination exercises in the 1980s, came to an abrupt halt after the Cold War had ended. In retrospect, the G•7 forum went through a glorious period during the years of the Reagan Administration in the 1980s, and it was hoped that the newly found initiatives in co-ordinating fiscal and monetary policies would continue well into the 1990s, after the breakdown of the Communist system had occurred. This, however, was not the case, since European countries initiatives were diverted towards their own goals in constructing a single currency, leaving the U.S. to pursue unilateral moves against Japan and the yen. For a brief few years after the ending of the Cold War system, the Bush administration accelerated its public criticisms of Japan's trade policy. They made the Japanese government, and its corporate leaders, look as deliberately trying to increase sales to the U.S. market, hence increasing the trade gap between the two countries. In return, the Japanese system of "keiretsu" was particularly singled out for criticism for not allowing an appropriate level of reciprocity to the "Big 3" producers. This, despite the fact that the U.S. auto producers did not have the appropriate type of product on offer for the Japanese market. The pattern in Japan was that consumers preferred cars that had a particular size of engine, and sales were broken down into this very specific type of buying pattern. The ironic aspect to the entire initiative, was that most of the U.S. auto producers, did not produce a product line that was a fit to this trend in consumer preferences in Japan.

The unilateral and confrontational trade initiatives directed against Japan by the Bush administration, earned the U.S. the "globocop" label, shortly after the Communist system disintegrated in 1990. For a brief several years thereafter, the U.S. found that its status as the only remaining superpower in the world became increasingly defined around confrontational economic initiatives with respect to Japan. The election of the Clinton administration in 1992 continued with the attacks over Japan, carried out by Trade Representative Mickey Kantor. During the period from 1992 to 1995, some of the most erratic swings in the history of the dollar/yen parity had occurred. On many occasions, traders synchronised these movements directly with trade rhetoric that came out of Washington, and which was reported by the *New York Times* or *Washington Post*. The global trade politics that emerged in the 1980s via the Plaza Accords in New York, were extended into the new era of globalisation in the 1990s; this time with much less negotiation and far more confrontation and unilateralism.

This brand of "currency politics" reached a climax when the yen hit ¥79 to one dollar in 1995, but did very little in plugging the trade gap as the Japanese surplus position persisted throughout.

The countries of the European Union showed little opposition to the confrontational unilateralism that the U.S. chose to pursue in its relations with Japan in the early 1990s. What is even more perplexing, is the posture that Japanese officials adopted throughout these years, preferring to accept the outcomes dictated by these "currency politics" that were promoted by first the Bush, and then the Clinton Administrations after the Cold War had ended. When spoken to on a one-on-one basis, Japanese executives of the larger companies dislike open discussion of any matters that have to do with trading relations with the U.S. Very often, the leaders of these corporations just tacitly accept the outcomes, and instead try to satisfy U.S. politicians by making job-enhancing direct investments in the U.S., as a conciliatory gesture for the large trade imbalances. Moreover, these same executives vehemently dislike open discussion, or any suggestions that have to do with the way in which the surplus dollar funds are re-channeled into U.S. Treasury bonds and bills. In short, the evidence points to an overwhelming passiveness on the part of both corporate leaders, as well as government officials, which includes the newly-independent Bank of Japan. In summary, any time the U.S. takes a political initiative against the trade surplus, Japanese leaders make conciliatory gestures by building new plants in the U.S., and by agreeing to hold U.S. bonds and bills.

After the over-reaction of the yen towards the ¥79 level to one dollar, U.S. authorities began to water down their rhetoric against the Japanese surplus. Further evidence began to emerge of the severity of Japan's downturn as the bursting of the "bubble economy" in the late 1980s, did not yet work its way through as it had in the U.S., U.K., Canada and even Europe. Japanese officials began to assert the fact that their economy seemed to be in a permanent state of deflation, whereas the other members of the G•7 were struggling with the milder form of disinflation. Deflation was a more severe adjustment on continuing downward pressures in prices, while disinflation had more to do with engineering price stability under the new system of globalisation. President Bill Clinton came to grasp the situation in his second term in office, and the rhetoric that was so much associated with his trade representative in the first term, Mickey Kantor, was all but missing in the latter half of the decade, thereby ending one of the more peculiar economic relationships in recent history.

Why traders continued to react to the trade surplus well into the new decade, had something to do with the slow pace in which Tokyo was integrating into the global financial market. It was only in the middle of the decade when Japanese authorities moved to liberalise the local capital and stock markets in accordance with international trends. Even still, there exist protectionist tendencies among governments, after both the local Tokyo government moved to levy a surtax on the profits of local Japanese banks, and the Liberal Democratic Party reconsidered closing any gaps on the withholding tax on foreign investors in the government bond market. The openness that is expected by the powerful three classes of investors in the 1990s, was not too clear in dealing with the Japanese financial centre of Tokyo. Had Tokyo developed as transparently as New York and London, then trade flows such as the constantly accumulating surpluses would not have mattered as much.

As Japan opens its markets and connects them to the global financial economy, the surplus position with the United States will have less relevance. Recent evidence with respect to the behaviour of the yen at the turn of the millennium, indicates that it has stabilised, and that the wild and erratic movements of the first half of the 1990s are all but over. However, should Japanese officials renege on the progress in making Tokyo an open and transparent financial centre of some importance, then the pattern could very well revert backwards to what was the case during the Kantor years in the first Clinton administration. The progress of the expanding bond market currently, will ensure that more and more foreign investors will be pulled into Japan, given that the U.S. and the U.K. are becoming budget surplus countries that no longer have such a requirement for issuing new debt. In that respect, Tokyo will become a financial centre of growing importance globally, as the draw of its huge debt market will require that the local authorities be pressured to maintain international standards of openness and transparency, so that the three classes of private investor- the new power in the global economy; be assured that their capital would not fall under any political risk.

Under this new era of open and liberalised financial markets in Tokyo, the U.S. government will have less reason to conduct "currency politics," as it has done on so many occasions and in so many varying degrees over the past fifteen years. Now, the stakes are much higher, as financial flows into the yen could be expected to exceed those in trade by an average of 99 to one. The enormous global potential of the growing Japanese bond market, and its support by G•7 based pension and investment funds, will make any rhetoric against the yen a very risky prospect. The outbursts by U.S. politicians against the trade surplus usually moved the yen to a level of strength in relation to the dollar, but now the outcome will be much less predictable. Anything can happen when financial flows expand as they have been throughout this era of globalisation, and if U.S. pension money is now increasingly tied up in Japanese yen bonds, any erratic movement in the currency could immediately destroy the value of these funds. If the yen is going to assume the role of having the backing of the world's largest government bond market, then a stable currency will be in the interests of all investors.

GO LONG ON THE EURO, SHORT ON THE DOLLAR AND BE NEUTRAL ON THE YEN?

Can one be daring enough to make a long term forecast of the three major currencies in a book? The short answer is yes! But, the more that globalisation combined with technology brings about more efficient, fast and furious markets, the more difficult it will be to make spectacular returns on long and short positions, as George Soros has found out in the latter part of the 1990s. There are just so many players conducting global capital flows today, such that the ability to discern a general trend becomes much more difficult to identify and act on. To begin with, a long position on a currency, such as the Euro, means that the investor expects it to appreciate. Conversely, a short position on a currency, say the dollar, means that an investor hopes to profit from it depreciating or going down in relation to another currency such as the yen. Over the latter years of the 1990s, cross border merger and acquisition flows have impacted the dollar, but trying to forecast an acquisition trend is one of the most difficult things that anyone can attempt let alone analyse its aftermath. Likewise, a direct investment made in the U.S. by a German company, by first committing to a community and then building a place of work such as a plant, along with hiring a management team, is also extremely difficult to plot on a trend line.

The best approach would be to say: "Cross border mergers and acquisitions have been at a record high, therefore, what are the signs that would indicate a slowdown over the next year or two?" Recent evidence of a more activist Federal Trade Commission (FTC) for one, especially its move to break up the powerful Microsoft, is a good reason to discount much future activity in the area of cross border mega-deals. Likewise, better international co-ordination with the European Commission's Competition Directorate, under Mario Monti, has created a new trend against monopolistic global deal flow most recently. This should force a lull in the recent moves to create corporations that are larger than governments, hence causing less demand in global currency markets for the U.S. dollar.

In the case of the direct investment component, the buoyant U.S. economy has been a natural magnet for German, French and British companies escaping their domestic markets, and having a desire to join in the spectacular productivity gains offered by the new high tech economy. As long as the U.S. is perceived as being able to offer better than average growth in returns on investment, then this trend will continue until European governments clearly act in adding such an element of dynamism locally. This may not be as far off as many fear, since recent moves by Germany and France, not to mention some of the leading Scandinavian countries, have shown a willingness and eagerness in transforming their old and tired production-dependent industries. However, for now, let us assume that direct investment will continue to support the dollar in the global currency markets. The remaining factor affecting the direction of the dollar, is global portfolio flows into the U.S. This is affected by "blue-chip" stocks on Wall Street for the equity component, and the rate of interest for the fixed-income or bond component that make up a given balanced portfolio. With the Fed over-reacting on the scare of inflation in the first half of the year 2000, it may be a good time to call for lower short term interest rates, which would send both stocks and bonds upwards. By contrast, the low rates that are currently on offer in Europe and in Japan, can only go upwards, thereby adversely affecting equity markets, but rewarding risk-free floating rate bonds.

In the case of the euro, the initial act of corporate treasury managers re-balancing their borrowing portfolios, and repatriating capital back to their home base, has over-sold the Euro in its first year and a half. This "structural" effect was to have been somewhat expected, with the reservation that the direction of the currency was not too well known initially. Once this process is complete, it should join together with a halt in the capital outflows inspired by the record cross border merger and acquisition activity directed towards the U.S. market in 2000. In all, the Euro seems set to recover its early losses over the longer term, as several major structural factors are reversed over time. Should both cross border mergers and acquisitions and foreign direct investment revert back to a trend of normality, then portfolio flows will be the major determinant of the euro/dollar parity. What would be the likely impact of having a preponderance of portfolio flows between the Euro region and the U.S.? For one, interest rates and pure economic factors would take on a more prominent role once again. A falling U.S. short term fed funds rate and a rising Euro rate would result in a stronger Euro, however, the effect from the equity markets would be the real question. With U.S. blue-chip stocks making up a higher proportion of investment portfolios, a falling rate domestically would exert a positive effect on this asset class. Would it be enough to offset the capital outflows that were inspired by the falling rate?

In the case of Japan, financial flows will continue to gain in importance over trade flows, reversing the predominant trend apparent in the 1980s and the first half of the 1990s. Under such a scenario, the Japanese bond markets will come to replace the U.S. treasury market as the major source of risk-free government paper made available to pension and investment funds. Cross border mergers and acquisitions will continue to play just a marginal role in Japan when it comes to capital inflows or outflows, and will be restricted to interest from U.S. and European companies that would like to acquire some type of distressed asset. Foreign direct investment will continue to dominate in the form of a capital outflow from Japan to places like the U.S. and the U.K. Also, trade will still come to play a far more important role in determining currency parities vis-à-vis the yen, than it does in the case of the U.S. dollar, while being somewhere between these two extremes when it comes to the Euro zone. Portfolio allocation and the rise of Japanese bonds will come to play the most important role in determining the value of the yen, the dollar and the euro. The substitution affect alone, as portfolio managers shift funds away from the dwindling supply of Treasuries and Gilts, will mean that the yen will benefit from more demand due to this foreign capital inflow. Likewise, the trade surplus is expected to continue into the future, bringing a net inflow of funds, despite a major proportion of these transactions being paid in U.S. dollars and re-cycled into what remains of the Treasury bond supply. Overall, barring any unseen changes to direct investment and especially to cross border mergers and acquisitions, the yen can be expected to stabilise and increase over time.

The mode of long term analysis of the currency markets can take on the above format, and can become a little more technical with the use of many forms of technical analyses. However, what is important is the emergence of so many transactions and factors that justify the exchange of capital internationally and across borders. It is no longer possible to take a credible stand based on just one argument such as trade flows, or for example, the huge balance of trade deficit that the U.S. continues to carry with it over so many years. Practical good judgment is now more important than ever before, in balancing off these four effects that are now driving global capital flows, and which collectively come to form the value of a currency parity.

CANADA AND THE DOLLAR

The 1990s have been even less kind than the 1980s to the Canadian dollar relative to the U.S. dollar. A long time ago in the 1970s, for a very short period of time, the Canadian dollar was actually a few pennies stronger than its U.S. counterpart. This occurred during the era of pegged exchange rates around 1970, just before the Bretton-Woods system was completely abandoned during the time of the Nixon administration. For most of the inflationary 1970s, Canada pursued a nationalistic economic policy, restricting foreign direct investment inflows and keeping a suspicious eye on what was happening south of its border. During this period, politics and economic policy was formed under the premise that Canada was a closed country, and that the period of rising oil prices could effectively be shielded from consumers by regulating the international market and creating what became known as a "made in Canada" price for a barrel of oil. The posture which the Liberal government of Pierre Trudeau opted to pursue during this time, was very much reflected by its actions in the oil and gas market.

The 1970s were very much a decade where commodity-producing countries were left in a respectable strategic position, in contrast to the resource-poor countries which needed to struggle with ridiculously high energy and commodity prices. Even local governments were singularly defeated over their pricing policies with respect to gasoline and energy. The Conservative government of Joe Clark was in power less than a year in 1979, when it introduced a budget which pushed local gas prices closer to world market prices, inciting massive protests. Ultimately, the Clark government was defeated in a non-confidence motion over gasoline, and the Liberals under Pierre Trudeau were once again resurrected from defeat.

The 1970s were also an era of large-scale capital projects; such as the Alberta tar sands, which held large reserves of heavy thick oil that was difficult to refine and distribute, and the massive investments in energy exploration conducted in the northern arctic regions. The Cold War system of fragmented regions, was very friendly to large, resource-rich countries such as Canada. Investors came to view these countries as carrying a real premium, based on the high standard of living that such an abundance could bring. Often, Canada and the Soviet Union were comparable to one another from the perspective of size and resource richness during this time.

During the 1980s, Canada became even more attached to the U.S. market, as exports as a component of overall income grew to about one-third, as the natural allure of a boom created by deficit spending by the Reagan Administration was very difficult to resist by most Canadian manufacturers. The boom-time conditions after the interest-rate induced recession in 1980, resulted in the dependency ratio rising in relation to the U.S. market. More and more, as the Liberal era of Pierre Trudeau was swept aside, and politics took on a more Conservative bend, very soon there was an unstoppable inertia which swept in formal free trade arrangements with the U.S. Aside from the local rhetoric in opposition to free trade with the U.S., the Conservative government of Brian Mulroney sensed that an era of more open global commerce was upon us, and that Canada would do well in moving quickly to protect its most vital market, the United States.

After the collapse of the Bretton Woods system of currency pegs in 1972, the

Canadian dollar was on an unending downward spiral in relation to the currency of its most vital trading partner, the U.S. dollar. Despite constant agitation among the Senators representing border states, every administration in the U.S. understood that without easy access to their vast market by Canadian exporters, one-third of all incomes could potentially be affected in some way. In addition, Cold War strategic interests also prevailed, as the U.S. needed Canadian cooperation in order to patrol the northern reaches of the arctic for any Soviet intrusions that could threaten the United States directly. The low dollar politics took on an inertia over the 1980s that was difficult to reverse, even though many Senate leaders in the U.S. Congress constantly received opposition from their constituents who had to deal with very competitively priced Canadian exports.

The difference between the two dollar parities in the period of the Cold War, when compared to the era of emerging globalisation in the 1990s, was that the Canadian dollar began to track the deflating prices of commodities in the latter period. This behaviour was not obvious during the Cold War period, especially when rising oil prices during the 1970s, resulted in a dollar which was weakening in relation to the U.S. dollar. Why did this happen and can it be explained by economic logic? If the Canadian dollar was dependent on the balance of trade during the 1970s, as many of its G•7 counterpart currencies were, then it made sense only if the trade balance with the U.S. was on a long term trend downwards. However, this was difficult to imagine, since Canada was a net exporter of energy products, such as certain grades of oil and natural gas to the U.S. market, especially during the years of the OPEC oil embargo in the late 1970s. However, despite this, the activity on the capital account of the Canadian dollar worked against it, as travel to the U.S. and abroad kept a steady demand for the Canadian dollar low.

Under the period of emerging globalisation in the 1990s, the collapse of Communism began to tie all of the "emerging market" countries together now in a single global marketplace, driven by advances in high technology and communications. This started the new decade off with a challenging dose of "disinflation" as Canadian commodities that were priced in international markets, were now being challenged by continuously lower-priced commodities of the former Soviet Union countries. Not only was world market oil and gas production now located in Alberta and the North Sea, not to mention the Arab countries, but it was also very plentifully available from Kazakhstan and Azerbaijan; the newly-emerging markets of the old Soviet Union. This was also the pattern for many other basic commodities that were traditionally mined, sending prices lower and battering the price of gold well below three hundred dollars U.S. for the remainder of the decade. As a general gauge of inflation over history, it is interesting to note how gold has behaved in the era of globalisation, as disinflation in some countries combined with outright deflation in others, to exert an overall impact on lower and declining prices in general on a basket of commodities.

The Canadian dollar went down with the price of commodities, as it pushed to record low levels inviting criticism along the way from commentators, and adopting the unofficial "Northern Peso" label from those most critical of its recent performance. As the Asian crisis hit in 1997, it spread to Russia and the central European emerging market countries in the fall of 1998, also affecting some members of the G•7 and Canada in particular. Having dipped below the important seventy U.S. cent point very briefly during the very close Québec Referendum of 1995, the ensuing emerging markets crisis in 1997 was notable from the perspective that the Canadian dollar was taken down simultaneously with the Thai Baht, Indonesian Rupee and the Russian Rouble. History was made, and Canada was distinct among G•7 countries for being the most vulnerable to such a crisis originating in the newly-emerging markets. Even an aggressive reduction in short term interest rates engineered by the U.S. Federal Reserve, could not save the Canadian dollar from its slide towards sixty U.S. cents.

The slide in the Russian Rouble preceded one of the biggest financial crises that the New York banking brethren has seen, and one of the most dangerous financial risks since the collapse of Barings bank. I refer to the near collapse of the Long Term Capital Management (LTCM) fund, which was directed by a group of star nobel prize winning academics and famed New York trader John Merriwether. Nobel prize winners Merton Miller and options pricing theory guru Myron Scholes were among the partners in the speculative fund that took positions based on historical financial relationships in the markets confirmed over time. The leverage that LTCM amassed was so great, and the individuals so influential to have received so much credit backing, that a turn for the worse during the emerging market crises stood traditional relationships on their head, and at the same time created an unprecedented situation of panic. So severe was the potential impact on the U.S. and the world financial system, that Federal Reserve Chairman, Alan Greenspan, took the unprecedented step of seeking help from all major global commercial and investment banks, along with an aggressive program to reduce short term rates, and add liquidity to U.S. and world financial markets.

Despite this crisis in New York, the consequences were felt more in the Canadian currency and stock markets in Toronto, than they were on Wall Street. The fears being that the deflation-ravaged domestic Canadian economy was about to absorb yet another dose of confidence-shattering crises. Such an event would destroy the consumer confidence that was so difficult to rebuild after the early 1990s commercial property crash, and several "double-dip" recessions thereafter. Immediately, the Canadian dollar followed the Rouble, Baht and Rupee downwards, much to the surprise of many investors. The crisis in Russia was particularly troubling, as many commodity exports such as oil and gas, were now far more competitive in global markets after the Rouble's collapse. Furthermore, the metal-based commodities that Russia exported impacted the Canadian economy directly, calling for a lower dollar in order to compete on international markets.

The 1990s began with a crisis at Canada's central bank, which was supposedly independent. Governor John Crow, appointed during the era of Brian Mulroney's government, was a devout monetarist and inflation fighter. He pursued an aggressive policy which was designed to enhance the credibility of the Bank of Canada, as an inflation-fighting institution. This policy was implemented by a combination of high real interest rates and an appreciating dollar, which was impacting the bottom-lines of the all too-important exporters in the manufacturing sector. The election of the Liberal government of Jean Chrétien in 1993, elevated the comments of Finance Minister Paul Martin Jr., which were very much anti-Crow and against the Bank of Canada's uni-dimensional pursuit of fighting inflation. Martin quickly orchestrated a campaign to remove Crow from the Governorship of the Bank, in favour of a mild-mannered career central banker, in the form of Gordon Thiessen. The severity of the downturn in the early part of the 1990s, was a good enough reason for the government to reject the harsh monetarist policies of John Crow, under a period where technological change would have made the entire concept of fighting inflation somewhat redundant anyhow. However, what was at stake under the Crow episode, was the entire concept of the role of an overly-independent central bank, that was too singularly focused on one thing; fighting inflation. It also brings into question the entire trend in the 1990s of independent central banks pursuing their own agendas among the industrialised and advanced G•7 countries, when rapid technological changes in the latter half of the decade would have been a natural hedge against price increases anyway. In essence, to have a double dose of rigid central bank independence, as well as technological change and heightened levels of competition, combined together, was just too much to handle for some countries like Canada.

Just how independent is the Bank of Canada? It is independent only up to a certain point, as the Liberals so vividly illustrated via the Crow affair. With an ailing economy for most of the 1990s, and with constant attacks on Canada's standard of living from abroad via the global marketplace, political expediency ruled the day. In this case, foreign investors also reacted with dismay, as the Crow affair ran so much against the mainstream investor logic on central banking independence, not only among the G•7 countries, but also among the emerging market countries which so much aspired to inherit independent central banks and sound currency policies. It can be argued that the continuing structural weakness in the Canadian dollar, was also very much due to the interference that the Liberal government chose to implement against the Bank of Canada, in the early part of this new decade of globalisation.

STERLING CIRCUS

For a very long period of time, the pound sterling was supported by a unique combination of production in the Midlands and North Yorkshire, and the financial powerhouse offering of the City of London. In the 1970s, Britain was an industrial powerhouse that was gridlocked by a powerful labour union. In many cases, union demands on industry in the 1970s were very much anti-technological change and advancement in orientation. The long time Assistant Editor of the *Financial Times* of London newspaper, Sir Samuel Brittan, recounted to us in detail the days of publishing under the siege of powerful labour. In the case of the printing press, British unions still insisted in performing tasks a second time, despite the fact that these activities were already being absorbed by automation. For example, the process of bundling or bagging a newspaper or magazine, when it came off the printing press and into its final product stage, was often repeated over again by a worker standing at the end of the printing press. The printers union in this case, resisted any modifications in its age-old production practices, but which were becoming a real detriment to the advancement of the U.K. out of its old industrial age.

The ascent of Margaret Thatcher's Conservatives in 1978, was almost manufactured in order to change the balance of power back in the favour of capital, and away and out of the control of the increasingly powerful labour unions of the 1970s. In this period, the U.K. economy went through oscillating boom-bust cycles that were very much prone to inflation. Consequently, sterling fluctuated wildly on global currency markets, reflecting the open nature of this island economy, as well as the price competitiveness of its exports. Margaret Thatcher's government came to define the 1980s, as the fiscal position of the government came closer to balance over time, and the momentum gained on the continent via a system of pegged exchange rates, began to gather political momentum in the U.K as well. Very soon, open discussion was engaged by commentators, journalists and opinion formulators in the U.K. on the likely

benefits of the U.K. joining this currency peg, and ultimately one day participating in the crowning achievement; a single currency itself in the whole of
Europe.

Within the Thatcher Cabinet, there were several high profile Ministers that
were pro-European, and more importantly, pro-single currency. Their arguments were justifiably based on the need to even out the constant boom-bust
nature of the U.K. economy. These Ministers were Nigel Lawson at the
Treasury, and Sir Leon Brittan, who was the Home Secretary at that time, and
who after his tenure in the government, went on to play a very prominent role
as a high ranking trade official at the European Commission in Brussels. When
the single currency lobby spread to the U.K. in the early to middle 1980s, the
Thatcher government became the focal point of the pro-single currency lobbying efforts. Influential Ministers such as Lawson and Brittan, tried to convince
the Prime-Minister and many who were considered to be marginally sceptical
about the entire project, to join the European Exchange Rate Mechanism. The
argument for doing so, was that the Bank of England and the Treasury would
buy credibility from the Deutsche Bundesbank in conducting monetary policy,
and would thus be able to count on external factors in reducing inflationary spi-
rals, and at the same time curtail union power in negotiating wage increases. A
fixing of the sterling exchange rate would effectively reduce the options on
what the non-independent Bank of England could do in terms of its monetary
policy choices and inflation rate.

As mentioned, sterling throughout the 1970s and the 1980s followed a boom-
bust cycle. When inflation was driven higher by a combination of price pressures and union negotiating power, the Treasury, which controlled a non-independent Bank of England, moved to raise rates and puncture the inflationary
bubble. Likewise, when property prices went up during boom times, mortgage
rates were raised, sending them spiralling downwards. Many advocates of the
single currency during these years, felt that a peg was the only way in which
the Bank of England could achieve an independent policy stance, after so many
years under the control of the Treasury and political influence. The fastest and
most sound way in doing so, would be to buy the existing credibility from the
highly successful Deutsche Bundesbank; probably the best managed central
bank in the history of the European region. Only then, would policy be taken
out of the hands of the inept local politicians, and the boom-bust cycle would
come to an end.

Treasury Minister Nigel Lawson tried to convince a sceptical Prime Minister
Margaret Thatcher that participation in the Exchange Rate Mechanism was a
good thing for just this fact. A sterling peg would ensure that labour negotiating power would be kept in check, and that incompetent politicians at the
Treasury, would not be able to re-inflate out of tight situations that required

hard choices for the country. This was exactly the kind of prescription for the U.K. that Margaret Thatcher liked to hear, thereby allowing the Treasury Minister to manage sterling in such a way so that it was allowed to float at a parity of three Deutsche Marks since 1987. Ultimately, Great Britain joined the European Exchange Rate Mechanism in October, 1990, under the aggressive promotion of the new Prime Minister, John Major. Sterling entered the Exchange Rate Mechanism with a six percent fluctuation limit on each side of the central rate, meaning that it was allowed to fluctuate by twelve percent, without being devalued or revalued in some way. It was thought that since Sterling was highly successful in the late 1980s in tracking the Deutsche mark and the Exchange Rate Mechanism, this success would continue in the 1990s after the peg of six percent was formally announced.

In a way, London was a victim of its own success in the late 1980s. The development of commercial property projects ranked right up with activity in U.S. cities during the massive boom. Expanding ambitious new projects such as Canary Wharf in the Docklands district, was a symbol of the aspirations that London held as an expanding global financial centre. Already, it had a large share of international financial transactions, as well as the Eurobond markets. Moreover, it was poised to become a leading player in financing the newly-emerging countries of central and eastern Europe.

However, the success of London in attracting global financial investment in the important commercial property sector came under attack, as the new decade began, and both deflation and disinflation were in the air after the opening of markets that were closed during the Cold War. The Gulf War in 1991, added to the general uncertainties, and soon investment dried up when the Canary Wharf project filed for bankruptcy, and became a symbol of the excesses during this period. The "bust" in the commercial property sector hit London hard, and was enough to dislodge sterling from its newly-obtained Exchange Rate Mechanism membership.

The G•7 Report, published on July 22, 1992, sent out the following warning to subscribers: "... as soon as markets become uncertain as to the political resolve of maintaining the parity, as is the present case with the U.K., faced with a deteriorating economy. Then Sterling will and has come under speculative attack. Ever since the election majority was gained by the Conservatives, the aspirations were such that the newly won political stability supplemented with a pro-business environment, would immediately provide economic benefits through this election "dividend." This has proved false, as Sterling has fallen from the immediate post-election high of 2.95 to the Deutsche Mark down to the bottom of the E.R.M. grid to 2.85 to the mark. In light of the continuous deterioration in the economy, the positive sentiment has been broken and the commitment to a fixed parity increasingly questioned."

Enter George Soros, and the announcement by Finance Minister Norman Lamont, that sterling is suspended from the European Exchange Rate Mechanism with immediate effect, on September 17, 1992, and the planned base rate increase to fifteen percent in its defense is irrevocably cancelled. One week before this crisis, *The G•7 Report* published the following advisory: "The worsening economic conditions in the U.K. are a testimony to the real pressures that can build-up when a government pre-commits to an overvalued fixing of the exchange rate level. As inflation falls further, real rates rise having serious repercussions on real economic activity and employment. ... The situation has so deteriorated that one industry leader after another has urged intervention by the government. The latest being Sir John Quinton- Chairman of Barclays Bank who did not see any end to the downturn until well into 1994. ... The great pressure of the real economic downturn in the U.K. has affected their credibility to commit themselves to the E.R.M. Consequently, the opportunity cost of investment in Sterling denominated financial instruments increased over the past month. This can be seen as yields on 10 year gilts rose from one percent to 1.3 percent vis-à-vis German bunds, leaving a perception that devaluation of Sterling is more likely."

The daily currency volume in London doubled from April of 1989, from $187 billion to more than $303 billion by April of 1992. With such an increase, the Treasury was virtually defenseless in trying to fend off currency speculators and George Soros. The casualty in the entire affair was Treasury Minister Norman Lamont, as the humiliated government of John Major was forced to reduce base rates to eight percent on October 16, 1992, followed by yet another drop to seven percent, after the tabling of the mini-budget on November 12. Base rates were now at their lowest point since 1978, and the U.K. has completely washed its hands from its experiment with a pegged sterling to the Deutsche mark.

After the abandonment of the fixed peg to the Deutsche mark, sterling was left to float, while the Bank of England adopted a system of inflation targeting. The Bank of England was now formally independent from the Treasury, and it chose to target an inflation rate between one and four percent per annum, as measured by the retail price index, excluding mortgage payments. As *The G•7 Report* reported on December 9, 1992: "The government has, however, announced that it would like to formulate its interest rate decisions around a basket of financial indicators such as money supply figures, asset prices and the exchange rate. ... the inflation rate will be targeted between one and four percent..."

With London being the most vital global financial centre, and with globalisation creating record capital flows, a fixed exchange rate is an extremely difficult prospect during periods of erratic volumes. This occurred in the early

1990s, and the timing for joining a pegged system of exchange rates could not have been worse. As foreign direct investment and cross border mergers and acquisitions accelerated in the latter half of the decade, the U.K's historical record of being a jurisdiction where capital could come and leave as it wished, created intense direct investment interest from U.S. and Japanese firms. They also were convinced that the early Exchange Rate Mechanism experiment with Sterling would ultimately lead to participation in the single currency, hence removing all export concerns and uncertainties from their currency risk models.

As it happened, the prelude to the launch of the single European currency in January of 1999, drove sterling back up to a level of three Deutsche marks, based on "fright capital" from the continent taking refuge in London. As it happens, those investors who were sceptical at the start have been right in the short term. The new Euro has underperformed all expectations, and those that moved assets into sterling have had a net currency gain in excess of thirty percent. Moreover, the higher rate of return on sterling assets as well as the emergence of direct investment and cross border mergers and acquisitions, have also tendered a net gain to sterling holders. London is also becoming the true focal point in the Euro zone, as it moves to consolidate its leading position by merging its capital market operations with institutions based in Frankfurt, or even Stockholm? The traditional advantages of London in the capital and Euro markets, has combined with its unchallenged advantage when it comes to the quality of life and interest that the city has to offer; a very difficult combination for an emerging financial centre such as Frankfurt to beat on its own.

FRENCH MYTH

Newly-elected Socialist President Francois Mitterrand did not hesitate to implement his now infamous "dash for growth" in 1981, sending the French franc spiralling downwards and creating what proved to be a momentary crisis in European monetary relations. Prior to this, a series of serious summits and meetings between the former French President, Valéry Giscard-D'Estaing and German Chancellor Helmut Schmidt, led both leaders to propose a course of action that would bring to an end the erratic and violent currency swings during the 1970s, and also react to the perceived weakness from the U.S. after the unfortunate chain of events which included the Viet Nam war, the O.P.E.C. oil crisis, and the general weakness of the administration of Jimmy Carter.

What emerged out of these meetings, was a framework for bringing some sort of order to the diverse conduct of monetary policy within continental Europe.

What both leaders acknowledged, was the devastating impact which the erratic movements in continental currencies have exacted on trade and overall growth. Both agreed that there must be some course in policy which could shield European countries from economic and financial shocks, such as the O.P.E.C. oil embargo in 1974. In 1978, the European Monetary System (EMS) was born. As Michele Fratianni and Jürgen von Hagen explained in their book, *"The European Monetary System and European Monetary Union,"* The EMS was created to "... strengthen co-ordination of monetary and economic policies among the members of the Community, to stabilize exchange rates, and to take a new step on the road of monetary unification in Europe..."

In fact, the European countries have a very long history of attempts at co-ordinating monetary policies. As early as 1959, the European Parliament proposed the formation of an institution patterned after the U.S. Federal Reserve System. A number of prominent European Community politicians, including Jean Monnet and Pierre Vigny, endorsed some form of exchange rate union. The European Monetary Agreement of 1958 strengthened the provisions of the Bretton Woods system by limiting the bilateral margins of fluctuation among the European currencies to three percent. However, the 1970s brought about a gradual erosion of the Bretton Woods system, and as its focal point, the U.S. dollar spiralled downwards under a series of crises. With the breakdown of the Bretton Woods system of pegged exchange rates, the external guidance for ordering European currencies went out the window, which was another incentive that spurned Giscard and Schmidt to create the European Monetary System. The entire concept of monetary co-ordination in Europe was actually proposed by German Chancellor Willy Brandt at the Summit of the European Council in the Hague on December 1969, but Giscard and Schmidt made the first serious attempt to implement Brandt's vision via a policy framework.

This political move by Schmidt and Giscard did not have the blessing of the European bureaucracy in Brussels, nor was the German Bundesbank informed on the attempts to create a permanent mechanism for co-ordinating monetary policy. Furthermore, Giscard came under heavy attack in France for having succumbed to what was perceived as "German national interests." Helmut Schmidt in his memoirs wrote: " Giscard developed this argument into a dimension of the 'Grand Strategy.' He characterized Britain as a power which could not rank with France both in economic and military terms, and called upon the French spirit not to be satisfied with being a secondary economic power, but to strive for parity with Germany. Should France miss this goal, Europe would be dominated by Germany." Giscard's attempt to re-position this agreement with the Germans as a direct economic challenge to France as well as being an unprecedented opportunity at the same time, established a very long term goal for France to psychologically attempt to keep up and surpass the

Germans economically. Only seventeen years later in the mid 1990s, would evidence begin to surface of France's superior economic and financial performance relative to Germany.

Francois Mitterrand quickly abandoned his experiment with unilateralism, as the franc came under immense pressures in relation to the dollar and the Deutsche mark, with very little to show in terms of economic improvement. Specifically, the "dash for growth" created an increase in public debt, which jumped from 9.1 percent of GDP in 1980, to fifteen percent in 1983. In addition, the money supply rose by 15.9 percent in 1981 and by 10.9 percent in 1982, and inflation was 12.6 percent, compared with 4.5 percent in west Germany at the time. However, the unemployment rate, a central theme of importance to the Mitterrand government, actually increased despite the stimulus, going from 6.5 percent in 1980 to 8.1 percent in 1982.

The impact on the franc in the European Monetary System was extremely severe, as it was devalued three times between 1981 and 1982, depreciating a total of fourteen percent in relation to the Deutsche mark, while the current account deficit increased by 2.2 percent of GDP in 1982. The government of Francois Mitterrand was left to embark on a program of austerity and control of the deteriorating current account, representing a total reversal in policy from the initial "dash for growth." in 1981. Except for this brief period in recent French economic history, one can effectively argue that France has kept pace with Germany far better than any other country in the European Union, and especially in comparison to the performance of the U.K.

For the remainder of the 1980s, the government of Francois Mitterrand held its own in relation to the Deutsche mark and the Bundesbank. In a way, many former French politicians were now leading figures at the European Commission in Brussels, and were in a position in order to articulate a vision for Europe. The accession of former French Finance Minister, Jacques Delors, as European Commission President in 1986, laid the eventual groundwork for the final road towards monetary union. The Delors Report of 1989 was adopted into the Maastricht Treaty for monetary union in 1991, and it was the first time where all of Europe's central banks were invited to contribute to the process for monetary union. The Delors report promoted the entire concept of "parallelism" where economic and monetary integration must be pursued at the same time, setting the stage in the 1990s for both economic deepening in Europe, as well as the single currency.

Everything in the late 1980s went well for France. The franc overcame its early setback after the infamous "dash for growth," and was now firmly at the heart of the institutions that made decisions for Europe. As the Cold War ended, and recession appeared in the early 1990s in the U.S. and the U.K., continental European countries were still living from the mini-boom that German re-unification created. The decision by Helmut Kohl to exchange the east German mark with the Deutsche mark on a one-to-one ratio, armed east German consumers with purchasing power which was unleashed in the west German retail sector. The boom created the now infamous episode of inflationary pressures, which lead the Bundesbank to raise short term rates above nine percent, hence creating the conditions for the currency crises in Italy and the U.K. The case of France was somewhat different, after falling into recession in 1992, the franc was not devalued in a dramatic fashion as in the case of the lira and sterling. Instead, pressures that had built up from speculators and hedge funds, were repelled by constant contacts at a high level between the Bank of France and the Bundesbank, not to mention political summits conducted between Kohl and Mitterrand.

It was decided in the summer of 1993, to widen the bands of the Exchange Rate Mechanism, by fifteen percent on either side of the central parity. This came after an unbearable period of pressure by hedge funds taking short positions on the franc. In fact, the man who became known for "breaking the resolve of sterling," George Soros, appeared in the media on the side of France. Soros claimed that the fundamentals in France with respect to its budget deficit and inflation rate, justified a strong franc and went as far as defending the current parity vis-à-vis the Deutsche mark. Despite this appeal from the most influential financier in this period, the franc had to be devalued officially. The extension of the bands of the Exchange Rate Mechanism to fifteen percent were, however, contrary to the Maastricht Treaty which stipulated a 2.25 percent band. Under such conditions, the single currency project in Europe was seen by many as fading away very rapidly during this early part of the decade. What was a very promising era during the 1980s for European economic and monetary union, quickly lead to a decade of recession, unbalanced business cycles among European countries and massive speculative currency crises.

In fact, the difficulties that were being experienced throughout this period with the timetable for monetary union, could mainly be blamed on the diverging business cycles in Europe and in Germany in particular. The shock that German re-unification imparted to the other members of the European Community was felt for many years to come. The artificial "mini-boom" that resulted from the over-optimistic conversion rate on east German marks, pushed by Chancellor Helmut Kohl, created havoc in the capital markets. The Bundesbank's policy of going it alone did not help matters as the steep rate increases had to be matched by France, if stability in the Exchange Rate Mechanism was to prevail. Despite the spectacular gains that France was making in its budgetary fundamentals and controlling inflation, the markets did not yet come to appreciate this side of the argument. France, for many, was still a society that was dominated by Socialist principles, and instead of dwelling on measures such as inflation rates and the declining budget deficit, these investors focused more on the rate of unemployment. As unemployment rose to record levels in the early 1990s in Europe, tension and continuous outcries from the powerful labour unions focused attention on the headlines of the daily news. It quickly became apparent that it would be difficult for the government to maintain a pegged exchange rate, under a deteriorating jobs situation. Moreover, it was this very fact that collapsed the fluctuation bands of the Exchange Rate Mechanism from 2.25 percent on either side of the central parity, to fifteen percent on either side, thereby suspending the main feature of the European Monetary System for a few years.

France was also making impressive gains on its corporate side, and was following a fast-track program in order to prepare all of its main corporate "jewels" for the new fast-paced era of globalisation. Only at the very end of the decade and into the new millennium would some of France's best known companies assume a leading role in the area of cross border mergers and acquisitions. Throughout 1998 to 2000, French companies continuously outpaced any other continental European country in participating in some of the largest "mega-deals" which were quickly coming to define its new industrial renaissance. Deals such as Renault's acquisition of Nissan Motor of Japan and the reformed Générale des Eaux's (now renamed as "Vivendi") acquisition of Canadian/U.S. media and drinks group Seagram, will be long remembered for its profound risk-taking ability and global innovation. At this very moment, the groundwork was laid for France's corporate sector to become a far more active player in the global sphere than did Germany's corporate sector. The capital outflows that these mega-acquisitions result in are vast, and the initiatives coming out of France, have accounted for most of the early weakness in the Euro, as their corporate jewels have turned in search for opportunities in the U.S. market.

At this moment, the transforming influence which the era of globalisation has had on the French corporate sector, is somewhat slow to materialise domestically. Even still, France remains as the fifth most important destination for direct investment. It ranks far below the U.K. in attracting corporate activity, but is about level with Germany in this respect. The transformation in the French corporate sector to one of the most aggressive buyers of U.S. based companies is expected to hit the domestic sector as well. Already, the government of Lionel Jospin is accepting that change is inevitable, and has adopted a "silent action" approach in this respect, as it must juggle the competing interests of the powerful labour unions, if it hopes to successfully reform institutions such as working hours and social benefits, not to mention the chaotic pension system.

Going back to the mid-1990s, it became apparent that the hard transformation of the French economy was beginning to bear fruit. The unemployment rate always stayed high, above eleven percent, but there were emerging signs of some positive developments in the economy. For one, management of the serious industrial companies began to talk openly of global warfare and competition. Many of the political cronies and appointees who came to define the 1980s, were shuffled aside and opportunities became open for very serious managers and executives. Moreover, the defense sector was forced to restructure under the direction of Jacques Chirac, as many family-owned firms such as Lagardère and Dassault, were forcibly merged into large public companies such as Thomson-CSF, and ultimately opened to global joint-ventures for the first time in history.

Another success story emerged in the automotive industry, as new production techniques were forcibly introduced in old jewel companies, such as Renault and PSV-Peugeot-Citroën along with Michelin. Most of the technology was viciously anti-labour, but the global trend towards a heightened state of competition required these types of actions, if these companies were to survive in the longer term. I remember meeting with the senior executive management of Renault in 1994, just when evidence was emerging that auto producers would have to adopt the world economy as their frame of reference in order to compete successfully. To this day, Renault has done so, but Peugeot-Citroën, has maintained more or less its regional European base, yet continues to perform very well with one of the most attractive product lines in the entire industry. Peugeot has demonstrated that it is able to withstand global competitive pressures to now, and still stay profitable via a regional strategy for the time being. However, there is a belief that in order to secure its long term future, it must act to establish some kind of distribution strategy in the enormous U.S. market.

Furthermore, the French banking sector has already done what both the Canadian and U.K. sectors are still only talking about- merge! The initial approach from Société Générale (SG) to absorb Banque Paribas, was quickly rebuked by Banque Nationale de Paris (BNP), which immediately tendered a competing hostile bid for Paribas. After a lengthy battle that went over several months, the hostile bid by BNP prevailed, and the assets of Paribas were absorbed into the BNP structure. SG was left to consider possible foreign or intra-European combinations to counter the newly-formed strength of BNP-Paribas. Further, Crédit Commercial de France (CCF) fell into the hands of global U.K. commercial bank, HSBC, and immediately forced the still independent Crédit Lyonnais to consider combining its assets with a grouping of Pan-European Italian and Spanish banks to ensure survival. With the restructuring in the domestic banking system almost complete, French banks are better positioned to assist the French "jewel" corporations in pursuing their global ambitions in acquiring foreign companies.

In a quick retrospect, France has gone from the early 1980s "dash for growth" period under the newly-elected Socialist government of Francois Mitterrand, to a period of reconciliation with its European partners in the latter years of the 1980s. As the Cold War ended and the Berlin Wall collapsed, a radical transformation was in the making, which would only yield visible gains in the latter part of the 1990s. The fact that France not only kept up to German performance, but began to exceed it in the latter half of the 1990s, dispelled any notions that France was still a slow-moving Socialist country that would never be on the cutting edge of anything. In short, the record has killed the "French Myth."

ITALY'S DOUBLE LIFE

During the Cold War period, Italy was a vital interest to the U.S. and NATO as it represented the southern European border with the Communist bloc to its immediate east. The Communist party played a powerful role, particularly in conjunction with Italy's major labour unions throughout this period, as the entire country was presented as a constant balance of diverse forces and special interests, of which any officially elected democratic government at any given point in time was itself just one of many competing factions. Italy was governed by a coalition of Christian Democratic parties and Socialist parties, with politicians Giulio Andreotti and Bettino Craxi, coming to define each respective political party. No other democratic country in the world, was known to have so many different governments throughout the Cold War era. The Christian Democrats under Giulio Andreotti were in power no less than seven times and if any one government exceeded a period of one year in power; it was considered to be a political record-breaking feat of major proportions in modern Italian political history.

Each faction in Italy operated under some form of protectorate, with the industrial interests of the Agnelli family and those of former Olivetti Chairman, Carlo De Benedetti and businessman turned politician, Silvio Berlusconi, governed by Milanese merchant bank, Mediobanca, while political power groups came to rely on southern mafias to ensure that they maintained the Communists out of office in the poorest regions of Italy, where their support was strongest. The privately-held industrial power groups, which were organised around the large automotive producer, Fiat, relied on a system that was mediated by the late Chairman of Mediobanca, Enrico Cuccia. This system, known as the "solotto buono" or the "good drawing room" was a system of capitalism that became defined by the Cold War period in Italy. Briefly, Cuccia was able to organise an industrialist's collective which protected itself from predators both within Italy, as well as external threats from European industrial competitors. More importantly, it was a very powerful union that offset and balanced-off the power of the labour unions, as well as the chaos that regularly gripped the government. To ensure that he had loyalty, Cuccia's club of industrial groupings organised a series of interlocking shareholdings similar in nature to Japan's keiretsu, that bound together one another's interests and which allowed them enough power to attack a "common enemy."

The 1970s reached a crisis point after the murder of Christian Democratic President Aldo Moro, by the radical left wing Red Brigades terrorist group. Chaos during this decade came in many forms, and tipped the balance of power away from the government and industry, and was generally in danger of destabilising Italy. Economically, the massive impact that the O.P.E.C. oil embargo had on the domestic economy, led to a series of forced devaluations in the lira. The overall chaos during the 1970s, prevented Italy from participating in the newly-created European Monetary System as an equal to France and Germany. Instead of adopting the 2.25 percent fluctuation band for the lira, Italy was forced to enter the system with wider margins of six percent on either side of the central parity. This continued throughout the 1980s, until on January 5, 1990, the lira formally adopted the narrow 2.25 percent band.

Italy found it difficult to recover from the ensuing chaos that it had to endure in the 1970s, and the 1980s were a period which forced the competing interests to come to some kind of terms with its external European obligations, which were at a high in popularity throughout the 1980s under the Presidency of Jacques Delors. However, it can be accurately stated that Italy was one of the most enthusiastic supporters of a single European currency right from the start. Many of its supporters who despised the internal factional system throughout the Cold War, desired some form of external discipline which would keep everyone in line. The monetary regime that was offered by Schmidt and Giscard d'Estaing in 1978, was ideal in the sense that the politically-influenced Bank of Italy would come under the direct influence of the rigours of the German Bundesbank, and its skills in managing inflation.

In the 1970s, the Italian Treasury was able to write its own cheque for its spending needs, via an overdraft facility with the Bank of Italy, which basically meant that governments during this time relied on printing new money to achieve their spending goals. Moreover, the Bank of Italy was forced to buy government debt at Treasury auctions, thereby expanding the monetary base even further, and the absence of secondary markets for this debt, prevented it from any hopes of neutralising these inflation-creating policies. According to Fratianni and von Hagen, the Treasury began offering its bonds to the public in 1976, hence setting up an opportunity for the Bank of Italy to conduct open market operations and control the rate of growth of the monetary base and inflation.

As Italy entered the European Monetary System and the exchange rate mechanism, a degree of external influence already began to erode the control which the politicians had over the Bank of Italy. In 1981, the government was forced to release the Bank of Italy from its obligations of buying Treasury bonds that were issued to fund spending programs. Furthermore, unions and employer organisations were forced to factor in the new "externalism" which was creeping into Italian factional life through its greater commitment to European ideals. Politicians would consistently use the European Monetary System, as an external argument in their moves to limit wage increases and not pursue export-enhancing devaluations of the lira, much to the anger of the industrialists. If there was ever a country that changed its internal system via external pressure, it was Italy within the whole context of pursuing membership in the single European currency. The institutional apparatus set up by Brussels was tempting, but at the same time far reaching in its impact on the factional system within Italy.

As the Cold War came to an end, Italy was mired in an unprecedented series of wide open corruption scandals, that positioned a group of Milan-based Magistrates on the leading edge of fighting political and industrial corruption. Lead by the authoritative Magistrate, Antonio DiPietro, what became known as the "Tangentopoli" exploded in allegations against some of the best known political and business figures in Italy. Carlo De Benedetti, formerly of Olivetti fame, was investigated, as was media tycoon turned politician, Silvio Berlusconi; who still to this day, almost ten years later, is fighting allegations of bribes allegedly offered to Magistrates and politicians in the 1980s. Not only this, but two of the most well-known political institutions in Italy, those of Bettino Craxi and Giulio Andreotti, were brought to justice over alleged corruption and mafia associations in the southern areas of the country.

The collapse of the Cold War and the opening of a global marketplace, together with the strengthening of European institutions, resulted in a complete breakdown of traditional political coalitions and factions in Italy. No longer did Italy require a buffer between the Christian Democratic party of Andreotti and the Social Democrats of Craxi, their Communist adversaries, and their alleged associations with the mafia families of the south, in order to mobilise votes and support in times of elections and maintain Italy within the democratic mainstream of Europe. Communism, which bound the political coalitions together with the mafias through so many decades after the second world war, was no longer a force in the geographical make-up of Europe, and at the immediate border to the east of Trieste. Moreover, the Magistrates who were very silent and discreet, during the height of the Cold War throughout the era of Ronald Reagan in the 1980s, were now free to pursue an agenda that would more closely match the new era of openness and change.

Bettino Craxi immediately fled and eventually died in exile in Tunisia, while Andreotti stayed in order to fight, in his own words, "the trial of my life," at the age of seventy-eight, eventually going on to win his case in a Palermo court, and clearing his name many years after the initial allegations surfaced in 1991. The only remnant of the fight with Milan's Magistrates, remains with Forza Italia leader Silvio Berlusconi, who effectively transformed himself into a leading politician, after founding the "Forza Italia" centre-right political movement in 1994, and going on to briefly become Prime Minister. Recently, Berlusconi won a case while in opposition, brought against him, where it was alleged that he bribed a Milan Magistrate to rule in favour of his company's takeover bid against that of a competing bid by rival industrialist Carlo De Benedetti, over the fight for control of the Mondadori publishing group.

The transformation from a local and factional country, to one that was opening up to European institutions was long and hard throughout the 1990s. The political and legal problems that surfaced, were joined by a very late economic transformation that was and continues to be very challenging. The difficult choices that were made by the U.S., Canada and the U.K. in the early part of the decade, are only now forcing adjustments in Europe, with Italy behind the trend. The adjustments forced on politicians to meet the single currency criteria by 1999, as set out by the Maastricht Treaty, forced Italy to reduce its national debt level from some one hundred and twenty three percent of GDP, to a level that would approach sixty percent. Likewise, the fiscal deficit position had to be curtailed from nine percent of GDP to three percent. A series of far-reaching tax increases were forced through Parliament by Romano Prodi and his party of the Democratic Left, to ensure that the Maastricht criteria were being addressed in an appropriate manner, and more importantly, to appease the lingering German opposition to Italy's early entry into the single currency club.

In his recent state of the economy speech, Bank of Italy Governor, Antonio Fazio, painted a bleak picture on the state of the Italian economy. He indicated that Italy's growth rate was seven percent behind the average European rate and that industrial production rose just ten percent between the hard transition years of 1994 to 1999, compared with sixteen percent for Europe. In addition, and what is more surprising, exports increased just twenty-four percent between 1995 and 1999, while those for the Euro zone increased by 41 percent. Despite this, unit labour costs increased six percent more than in the Euro zone. The Bank of Italy is openly fearful of the hard transition that Italy forced itself into, when Germany always believed that an appropriate level of convergence with regards to the Italian economy was always absent. The irrevocable pegging of the lira seems to have inflicted a real setback on the export sector, after it was one of the most vibrant performers in the period of the early 1990s, just after the lira was bounced out of the Exchange Rate Mechanism and was trading largely devalued.

Italian fashion, design and style remains second to none in its global appeal, and a natural force that will ensure that the trade balance will always be in Italy's favour, despite these recent setbacks as reported by the Bank of Italy. Brand names such as Ferrari and Maserati in automotive production to Bulgari and Armani in high fashions, Italy is one of the best positioned European countries to benefit from brand name recognition globally. The transformation that is occurring will see a structural re-organisation among the exporting sectors, that will need to cut costs to maintain a competitive position in some product fields. However, the luxury brands such as those mentioned here, will continue to create a global market despite the financial conditions that will determine pricing. The absence of the lira, will affect more the smaller sized producers that manage staffs of ten to twenty employees, and who are more based in the northern cantons of Veneto and along the Swiss border.

The fashion business, combined with the design and style sectors has always played a role in Italy's business infrastructure, even during the height of the chaos that afflicted the country throughout the 1970s. Underneath the competing factions in government, industry and labour, that came to define the country during the Cold War years, were these sectors that produced a highly desirable fashion culture which was exported and emulated globally. What is interesting now, is that the era of globalisation and European participation, has held in check the special interest groups that have so come to define the Cold War period, and has revealed the beauty that makes up the foundation of modern Italy, and a beauty that has always transcended the two eras that both preceded and followed the collapse of the Berlin Wall.

THE G•7 AND EXCHANGE RATES

The G•7 members including the U.S., Canada, Germany, France, Italy, Japan and the U.K., with the latter inclusion of Russia, have always been a fiscal and monetary policy information forum. Only for a very brief period of time since its creation, did the G•7 actually co-operate to co-ordinate the direction of economic activity. Central to the whole concept of policy co-ordination is controlling wildly fluctuating exchange rates among the world's major industrialised countries. Adverse exchange rate movements distort international investments, as well as strategic planning initiatives, while creating uncertainty and project delays. Based on the premise that it is good to control the fluctuation of exchange rates, a good beginning would be to co-ordinate fiscal and monetary expansions among a grouping of countries. If the G•7 moved in tandem to expand money supply by ten percent, meaning that money supplies in dollars, euros, yen and pounds sterling went up by ten percent, inflationary expectations would be the same in all of the G•7 countries and there would be no real effect on exchange rates. However, if the G•7 decided to expand money supply by ten percent, with the exception of Japan; preferring to hold its growth to zero, then the yen could appreciate by ten percent relative to the dollar, pound sterling and the euro. This latter unco-ordinated approach would cause havoc in global currency markets, hence distorting investment and trade. In short, it should be avoided.

The historical development of the G•7, must be traced back towards the development of the Bretton Woods System of pegged exchange rates after the second world war, and was influenced by one of the most well known economists in modern times, John Maynard Keynes. Where Bretton Woods ended off in 1972, during the peak of the Vietnam crisis, the European Monetary System tried to take over the function of coordinating monetary policies. Both the Bretton Woods system and the European Monetary System are fundamentally different from the G•7. Whereas the former two are formal agreements to coordinate monetary policies and inflation rates by fixing exchange rates, no such formal agreement exists within the G•7. In that respect, the G•7 is a forum that idealises the concept of coordinating policies in three different trading blocs throughout the world. However, there is no enforcement mechanism that forces its members to pursue monetary policies based on some form of pre-arranged fluctuation band for the group of currencies, and there is no assurance of success, given that no member is obliged to follow the final communique's that are issued at the yearly summits and through the more informal gatherings of Finance Ministers throughout the year.

In Europe, monetary policy coordination has a long history that predates the famous Schmidt-Giscard d'Estaing agreement to formally establish fluctuation bands in 1978. It was as early as 1959, that the European Parliament proposed the formation of an institution patterned after the U.S. Federal Reserve system for the purpose of coordinating monetary policies in Europe. The European Monetary Agreement of 1958 strengthened the provisions of the Bretton Woods system, which was already in place and functioning. However, the Monetary Agreement of 1958, proposed that the bilateral margins of fluctuation among the EC currencies be limited to three percent.

At the same time that the European Community decided to "harden" its commitment to monetary coordination practices alongside its commitment to the Bretton Woods system of pegged exchange rates, the Bretton-Woods system was under severe strains. The gold standard under which its central currency, the dollar was based on, began to slowly unravel in the 1960s at the height of the Vietnam war and the spending commitments made for the arms race, together with the strains of Lyndon Johnson's Great Society programs, proved to be too much for the system to bear. By 1968, gold convertibility at $35 per ounce had virtually ceased, when President Richard M. Nixon moved to formally end it on August 15, 1971.

In 1969, the French franc was devalued and Germany allowed the mark to appreciate, while a wholesale unravelling began the process that would see the eventual demise of the Bretton Woods system. In 1973, the United States itself, the anchor currency in the Bretton Woods system, announced a ten percent devaluation of the dollar, hence formally ending the international experiment of currency management which held together since the second world war.

The demise of monetary co-ordination in the 1960s, culminating with the French devaluation and the German revaluation, put enormous strains on the European Community, which considered monetary coordination a vital element in furthering the twin goals of political and economic union. After the crisis with the franc, mark and dollar began to appear, German Chancellor Willy Brandt, put forward an idea for monetary union at the summit of the European Council in the Hague in 1969. This lead to several attempts to coordinate exchange rate fluctuations, resulting in the "snake" agreement in 1972. However, this was short lived, as the O.P.E.C. oil embargo and the general inflationary environment during the 1970s, caused severe fluctuations in exchange rates, chaotic policy initiatives and desperate political manoeuvring in Europe, to cope with the rising energy costs.

In 1978, German Chancellor Helmut Schmidt and French President Valéry Giscard d'Estaing, created a new initiative that would establish the enduring European Monetary System and a formal Exchange Rate Mechanism (ERM), which would govern fluctuations among European member currencies tied to fluctuation bands of 2.25 percent on either side of the central parity for some countries, and six percent trading bands for other countries that were not considered to have a good inflation record. This was the final solution that eventually yielded a single currency and one European Central Bank.

The G•7 has at its core this incredible accomplishment among its European members, that moved a loose framework for policy coordination, into outright monetary union. Certainly, the G•7 never moved to replicate what had existed in the Bretton Woods framework of pegged exchange rates prior to 1969. For whatever reason, the G•7's agenda was a far more informal mandate to loosely exchange information and to act only when periodic financial crises arise in the global financial system. In essence, the G•7 has admitted that what has worked among its European members, can not necessarily be extended to include countries located among three diverse trading blocs around the world.

The glory period for the G•7 culminated in the Plaza Accords, negotiated in New York in 1985, and formalised two years later in the Louvre summit in France in 1987. The growing trade deficit in the U.S. automotive accounts with Japan, required a revaluation of the yen and Deutsche mark and the devaluation of the U.S. dollar, which lead to a new trade equilibrium in this turbulent period. Never again has such a high level of cooperation been noticeable, as the new era of globalisation presented an interesting new set of challenges. With deflationary conditions prevalent in the early 1990s, the "Anglo-saxon" grouping of countries that included the U.S., Canada and the U.K. were experiencing a sharp adjustment and a severe downturn, while the continental European members were experiencing a boom from German reunification. Under such a period of "structural" change, it was difficult for these two groupings of G•7 countries to be on the same point in their respective business cycles, hence unwilling to pursue any coherent form of policy coordination that made any sense.

For example, if the "Anglo-saxon" group of countries had argued for an expansion in the money supply or in fiscal spending, it would be, and was countered with a negative response from the inflation-conscious German Bundesbank. The fact that globalisation brought naturally diverging responses in the 1990s, made the whole mandate of the G•7 somewhat redundant. How could policy be effectively coordinated in light of each country being at opposite ends with respect to its business cycle? Moreover, there did not seem to be any room for any compromise or middle ground either, which was probably the most disappointing part of the failure to take an active role in policy coordination among the members of the G•7 during this period.

The 1990s have become a decade of open capital flows, budgetary surpluses and less active monetary policies. The role of the G•7 is now more important than it was ever before, during the closed economic era of the Cold War. Speculative pressures are now far more prevalent than at any time after the second world war, and many respected world leaders have called for some form of control in global currency markets. Many have even called for a reinstatement of the old Bretton Woods system, that would be much more far-reaching than the European Union was in establishing the Euro. The difficulty with any such moves, however, has to do with the divergence of interests of members in terms of where they are in their respective business cycles. As in the early 1990s, Germany wanted to see a decrease in spending, while most other recession-plagued countries called for an expansion. This kind of coordination is redundant in the world of growing global capital flows, which would create severe speculative pressures on currencies if such an imbalance were allowed to proceed at the policy end.

The hope that remains in coordinating business cycles, is the expansion of the information economy, even in countries on continental Europe which have realised that the rigid labour structures that have come to define this region, will inevitably need to disappear over time. These are the kinds of "structural" impediments which make co-ordination of policies very difficult, but which have the potential to lay a framework for a successful G•7 agenda over the next five to ten years.

TRANSITION TO WAR

The transformation from the Cold War system towards an open global economy was not always conflict free in the early years of the 1990s. The Berlin Wall went down, and eastern Germany began its long road of integrating its political and economic institutions with the standards dictated from the successful western region of the country. To this day, despite the favourable conversion rate that was offered by the then Chancellor Helmut Kohl to citizens of eastern Germany, and despite the billions of dollars that are still flowing into this region, unemployment rates remain stubbornly high and twice the levels evident in the western parts of Germany. The transition, which many thought would elevate the standards of the east to those of the prosperous west in a very short period of time; some estimates ranged anywhere from one to three years, are still on-going and to many standards are still inconclusive, despite the billions offered in infrastructure investment over the past decade.

The fastest change from a state-controlled economic system to a freer market economy, can be evident in the more successful countries in central and eastern Europe. Yet still, signs of success are variable even among the Czech Republic, Hungary and Poland. The creation of capitalist financial institutions such as stock exchanges, independent central banks and hard currencies has evolved in varying degrees in these countries, with each progressing to such an extent where they have become the preferred first round membership candidates for the European Union. Poland has accomplished a high level of transparency in the construction of its stock exchange and equity markets, with high levels of volume evident in the trading and brokerage operations among its members. Furthermore, many local Polish banks are in joint ventures, or have gained a major U.S. or European bank as a minority equity partner. Some have even been acquired outright by foreign financial institutions.

The defining developments for the Czech Republic are mainly connected with its proximity to major western European trade routes. Within easy reach are the major Austrian cities of Vienna and Linz, together with Nuremberg and Munich in the south of Germany. The Czech Republic has a very long trading tradition with these more developed regions of southwestern Europe, which has always included very close supplier links with some major manufacturers like Volkswagen and Siemens. Despite this, the Czech financial transformation has not gone as smoothly as Poland's, and the voucher scheme towards privatisation has been plagued with countless setbacks and corruption among politicians that were in charge of promoting and administering it.

Hungary was also one of the better positioned countries to welcome the transformation towards free markets and more openness in its economy. It has had a long and established tradition of experimenting with free markets during the Soviet era, and many of its local institutions reflect this. For a landlocked country at the border point near eastern Europe, Hungary's local economy has performed exceptionally well. The defining feature of most of these transitional countries in central Europe, has been the degree of openness of their financial sectors, as old state-controlled banks were required to shut down, transform themselves, or take the quick route by seeking a foreign acquisition or joint venture partner. The story on the real side of the economy, or when production was taken into consideration was very different. Most of the state-controlled industries that produced traditional items for the local market, were bankrupt as instantaneously as the old regimes fell. They continue to be nurtured by the new governments, and many continue to receive subsidies almost ten years after the initial transformation. Many are small and medium sized, and produce products that are more and more irrelevant to the global economy, and specifically to the economies of the European Union. A quick glance at the privatisation lists reveals that many of these companies produce products such as pencils, wooden furniture and low quality textile products. In a new era of freer trade and accession to the European Union, these industries would not have any chance of surviving against their competitors, who produce better quality goods that are recognized by brand name through advertising.

Even those firms that still have a market presence and are producing a vital necessity such as oil and gas, food or telecommunications, their managements are often still so inflexible that change has not occurred in their respective organisations, despite the changing economic and geopolitical climate in Europe. This stubbornness on the part of these managers, has prevented a quicker transformation in these countries, but admittedly, there were often times when unemployment had to become the overriding concern that governed how quick the change would affect these firms. However, to this day, many companies in central Europe are still managed by archaic managerial structures, with very little flexibility shown in accepting new procedures or more importantly, new talent. Many companies are governed as some form of "fiefdom" that is managed in a clan-like fashion, inflexible to outside ideas, and certainly not welcoming to ideas that would be passed along by professional consultants.

In many cases, even those former communist companies that successfully obtained a stock market listing, are notorious for neglecting the spirit of shareholder rights. Only a handful of truly global firms that are cross-listed on the local stock exchanges and in London, New York or Frankfurt, have anything resembling an appropriate conduct towards their shareholders. In many cases, even companies that are notoriously poorly managed and loss-making, are often very difficult to acquire over the stock exchange and effectively integratable into the operations of an acquiror. Despite this, investors must come to terms with the fact that central European countries, even the successful ones awaiting entry into the European Union, are still a part of the local social fabric and customs and culture of their respective countries. In no way are they open to the ways that govern business relations in the major financial city centres in the world. We must remember that a Hungarian company chooses to do business in Hungary or from Hungary, and not from London or New York. There is a major difference here.

As we move to the south of the success zone of Hungary, Poland and the Czech Republic, the transformation gets more difficult towards the new global system. Yugoslavia was once a shining example of how a Socialist country should be governed and economically organised. Under the dictatorship of Marshall Tito, it was known for its relative degree of openness throughout the Communist world, always ready to supply very cheap labour to German industry and the service sector, and its relative openness in economic and trading relations with Austria and Italy. Internally, the country was made up of a number of ethnic groups who more or less lived in definable regions such as Slovenia, Croatia,

Bosnia and Hercegovina, Serbia and Macedonia. The two of the northernmost Republics of Slovenia and Croatia, always had a good industrial base in relation to the other parts of the country, and the coastal region of Croatia was a much needed source of hard currency from the yearly tourist trade.

The 1970s were a glorious period in economic and political relations for Yugoslavia. There was economic growth, tourism and aid from the U.S. Congress, a prize for not falling too close within the sphere of the die-hard communist leaders in the Soviet Union. The internal ethnic divisions, especially between the Croats and the Serbs, were tolerable while the dictator Marshall Tito remained in power, and as long as economic growth continued to create acceptable prosperity within the country. After the death of Marshall Tito in 1980, and the accession of Mikhail Gorbachev in the Soviet Union, during the final years of the Cold War system, the old time ethnic divisions within Yugoslavia began to resurface. The greater competition and openness in trading regimes abroad and the fall of the vital middle-eastern oil markets, had an economic impact on some important industries in the country. Furthermore, the central bank was known to pursue quick solutions to the growing budgetary problems, which were called on to fund pensions and social spending schemes. The latter years in the 1980s, became known for hyperinflation and worthless dinars, which were pitched into the fountains throughout Zagreb by the handful, from quiet passers-by.

Yugoslavian industry during these years failed to pass on their foreign export earnings to the central bank in Belgrade, opting to unofficially trade in German marks and Austrian Schillings on their respective balance sheets. As economic conditions deteriorated further, so did ethnic divisions throughout the country. The conduct of business relations from the years 1985 to 1990, was oriented towards external trade, and was deteriorating rapidly among the internal Yugoslav Republics. It used to be that the production supply-chain in Yugoslavia was a web of interwoven economic relations among the various republics. Inputs would be produced in Slovenia, which would gain value-added in Serbia and then passed on to the final product stage in Macedonia. It was this economic network that bound the country together. In addition, hotels on the Adriatic Sea, which were a very popular vacation spot for western Europeans, began to withhold foreign exchange earnings repatriations to the central bank in Belgrade, adding even further tension to the situation. Once on a trip to Belgrade from Zagreb in 1989, the Zagreb Stock Exchange delegation that I was with, could not find a bank that had enough dinars for withdrawal on hand upon our arrival in Belgrade, and given that electronic credit cards were still quite rare in these parts during this time period, finding enough cash to meet our spending needs took up an entire afternoon. The situation was just as bad in the other Republics, as people spent cash as quick as they received it just to try to keep up with inflation.

If there was an economic case to be made for the breakup of the former Yugoslavia, we were witnessing and experiencing it first hand. What is more, the general mood within these Republics was a rare mixture of elation and doom. In Croatia, the people were very much in favour of independence, but the fear was that the traditional animosities with the Serbian people would resurface once again. A good number also felt that a break up of Yugoslavia would carry an enormous price with it; as it turns out they were right. The Yugoslav army became enraged at the thought of territory leaving the Federation, and in 1991 launched a symbolic attack against the northern most Republic of Slovenia.

Meanwhile, it was interesting to note that despite the ensuing political and military crises, the business communities tried to pursue business as usual under impossible situations. The money markets were trading at punishingly high rates of interest, that at one time, right at the peak of the military hostilities throughout 1992 and 1993 in Croatia, it was not uncommon that the best companies would borrow at interest rates above fifty percent over a one year period. And indeed, many were resilient enough that they were able to repay such punishingly high rates of interest on their business operations. These were companies that were mainly involved in the provision of necessities, such as the oil and gas sector as well as food processing. What was even more remarkable is that these money market rates of interest were kept high despite a general absence of hyper-inflation. Yes, there certainly was inflation, but the real rates of interest still accounted for some twenty to thirty percent of what was quoted. Moreover, there was precious little foreign capital that was flowing into Slovenia and Croatia from 1990 to 1994, at the peak of the crisis, that then migrated in a very brutal way towards Bosnia and Hercegovina. Even the border states of Austria and Italy were not so interested in investing capital in these volatile neighbours.

It took these countries almost a decade, a lost decade to many, to recoup the standard of living that they enjoyed during the peak of the former Yugoslavia in the 1970s. Not only did the decade of the 1990s bring about a new and more open system of doing business, it also brought revolutionary new technologies and the internet, while at the same time a brutal war, the effects of which will linger for at least another decade. Judging the progress of the breakaway Republics from the former Yugoslavia, the small alpine Republic of Slovenia is best positioned to become a member of the European Union. In many ways, Slovenia can be considered to be an extension of southern Austria, with a standard of living that is very similar. Today, when representatives from the European Commission in Brussels discuss enlargement of the Union, Slovenia ranks right up with Poland, Hungary and the Czech Republic.

The status of Croatia is somewhat more volatile, but the central bank under the governorship of the technocratic Marko Skreb, has done an admirable job in maintaining the new currency, the Kuna, stable and resilient to the up and down fortunes of the business community and tourism receipts. It seems as though tourism has finally returned to some degree of normality after ten years, and Europeans from the U.K., Germany and Italy, are once again making the Adriatic their choice of vacation spot on the Mediterranean Sea. The defeat of the nationalist Tudman government, has also gone a long way in opening up the country to foreign investors, and has been rewarded by Stability Pact grants from Brussels. Further friendly aid is expected to continue to supplement a general improvement in the overall business sentiments in this country, and the development of new venture capital projects and influx of lower priced loans and credit should boost overall economic activity.

The good news for the Balkans and the countries of the former Yugoslavia stops there. The jury is still out, however, on the progress of Bosnia and Hercegovina. After the negotiation of the Dayton Peace accords in 1995, it was always commonly believed that the then Croatian President Franjo Tudman and his Serbian counterpart, Slobodan Milosevic, have secretly agreed to carve up what currently remains of Bosnia and Hercegovina, and to annex these territories as parts of a greater Croatia and greater Serbia. As the country currently stands, it is a mish-mash of regional governments. First, there is the Hercegovinian region in western Bosnia that is economically and politically influenced by Croatia, while Republika Srpska, in the eastern region, bordering the Croatian region of Slavonia, is supported by Serbia. The capital, Sarajevo, is under muslim control, and there is anything but efficient contact and trade relations throughout. The country remains under the heavy influence of United Nations peacekeeping forces, while its official economy is mainly fueled by various forms of reconstruction grants by institutions such as the European Bank for Reconstruction and Development, and a raging black market.

Recently, there was some initial movement that inspired some hope, as some marginal investments were made in the private sector banking system by profit-oriented Austrian and German banks, for whom Bosnia and Hercegovina has always been of historical economic importance. Moreover, the large German multinational manufacturing companies such as Siemens and Volkswagen, have arranged a presence in the region, delivering positive economic gains by paying employees in hard currency. It is going to have to take some very strong economic activity to integrate the various parts of this country before peace-keeping troops could permanently leave, if ever.

The Republic of Macedonia is in an unfortunate position, as it must struggle against its land-locked geography, with wars recently raging in neighbouring Kosovo to the north, and utter chaos in Albania to its immediate west.

Moreover, the conflict between Serbia and Montenegro is unfortunately also within its geographical vicinity, with the consequences from this not yet known. The break-up of the former Yugoslavia has harmed this country a great deal, and the ties that its industry had at one time in the overall Yugoslav production chain, is no more. However, like any small Republic that is land-locked in Europe, it must adopt a strategy to develop a reputation as being good for doing something in a sector where it may have some sort of comparative advantage. Its very difficult to compare this country with Luxembourg and Liechtenstein, but these are yet even smaller, land-locked states which have created prosperity for their citizens by exploiting an advantage in the provision of banking services. If there is a political will to advance the living standards of Macedonians, politicians must act to follow a similar strategy, but at a much greater level of intensity.

The remaining Republic of Serbia, or Yugoslavia, as it likes to be called still, is the exception to the general rules of the new system of globalisation. A decade of wars and Slobodan Milosevic, has forced the remaining business community to go underground, and become involved in black market activities by necessity. The fact that Serbia refuses to become a part of the new economy and the mainstream, rejecting all facets of foreign direct investment as a form of meddling; continues to exert a punishing blow against the standard of living of all Serb citizens. Should Croatia succeed in its experiment of attracting foreign investors, and becoming a member of the European Union, along with the benefits of raising its standard of living, I am of the firm belief that Serbia would also opt to reap the benefits of a global market shortly thereafter, with the precondition that a more modern political regime is in place.

In 1991, "shock therapy" was advised by many reputable economists and institutions such as Harvard University in the west, as being the best route for the former Soviet countries to adopt a market style economy and integrate in the new global economy. Jeffrey Sachs became the best known advocate of this approach, which in retrospect, seemed to work the best in Poland, but failed to deliver what was promised in Russia and the Ukraine. Shock therapy was simply an approach that would allow unprofitable firms to go bankrupt without any more state aid, and would immediately open up these countries to western imports and competition, as a long term benchmark for local firms to aspire to in terms of both price and quality of the superior products that were being imported. It was believed that the global market would immediately plug the gaps in these countries, and offer enough foreign direct investment to replace all of the factories that were outdated and inefficient, and were remnants of the old system. I remember that a number of prominent economists during the early years of the 1990s also believed that there were some countries that would flourish under competition, while others would be bogged down in an eternal form of chaos, black market activity and organised crime. Among those that I spoke with, a consensus emerged that countries such as Romania, Bulgaria and the Ukraine would witness the most difficult transition. They were right. Romania has been struggling under the new system, as it still relies to a very large extent on traditional industry such as mining, which has long since been slowly in decline in the new era of rapid technological change.

Another characteristic that indicates the primitive nature of the process of development in these countries, is the importance in which the balance of trade surplus still plays a role in their overall budgetary strategies. In the case of Romania, it is this trade surplus which is constantly called upon to pay off the country's I.M.F. borrowings. The Ukraine is even more prone to these constant crises, as it struggles to shut down a good part of its dangerous nuclear industry. On the other hand, Bulgaria has made some noticeable gains recently, particularly with its management of its banking and financial sector, not to mention the stability that the currency, the lev, has inherited after the imposition of a "currency board" style of monetary system, which has more or less tied the hands of the Bank of Bulgaria to the actions of the European Central Bank. In short, what a currency board does, is allow the central bank to expand its money supply only when it is backed by a sufficient stock of foreign exchange reserves, which forces the country to run a trade surplus, or open up sufficiently to allow foreign direct investment and the acquisition of existing local companies which carry a market value. The capital inflow under these circumstances allows a one-to-one expansion in the domestic money supply. To now the Bulgarian currency board program has been a limited success.

In the case of the largest former Soviet country, Russia, the transition has been the most difficult, riddled with a number of political coups along the way, along with a visible rise in dangerous activity and mafia gangs, Russia has struggled to develop an all-embracing transformation to the new global economy. After the emergence of some evidence of stability, foreign investors piled into stocks listed on the Moscow stock exchange by the middle of the decade, adding upward pressure to the rouble. When the crisis hit emerging markets in Asia, it spread to Russia the year after, sending the rouble in a free-for-all, and causing countless numbers of foreign investors and funds to lose a good portion of their capital.

As in most panics, there is never a sound reason for why it occurs. Even experts at institutions such as the I.M.F. were caught completely off-guard by first the Asian crisis in 1997 and then the Rouble crisis in 1998. In retrospect, most of it had to do with a lack of development in their respective local financial markets. As in the case of Thailand, the government was forced to play Russian roulette by not having a locally well-developed bond market in order to borrow for programs and general expenditures. It accessed the U.S. dollar capital markets for its funding needs, but when the Baht collapsed, it was left holding obligations to its U.S. dollar lenders, that all of a sudden were exponentially more dear than when they were negotiated. The crisis became more serious as default loomed, spreading to other areas of the world with obligations outstanding that were rated less than triple A, under a general climate of panic in global markets.

The Russian rouble crisis eventually stabilised, but countless borrowing and bond obligations needed to be rescheduled to take into account Russia's rehabilitation of its battered financial system. To this day, Russian development continues to be characterised by a combination of organised crime, black market activity and the operation of the global market system. Where "shock therapy" in the early part of the 1990s failed, organised crime and black market activity are continuing to plug the gaps. The transition period has been a difficult one for these countries, but in the new global world, where private investors set the agendas for economic activity, the newly-emerging markets will have no choice, but to plug into this growing global pool of capital, if they desire a "world class" standard of living.

GLOBALISATION AND ORGANISED CRIME

The breakdown of the old Cold War structure caused tremendous displacement among the newly-emerging market countries in central and eastern Europe. Many of the managers that were entrusted to set five year plans for their enterprises during the Soviet era, were now faced with an entirely new set of rules that for many meant different things. Shock therapy, as advocated by many U.S. based economists in the 1990s, did not produce the desired results for these countries. To a very large degree, the fall in aggregate demand during the 1990s in the anglo-saxon grouping of countries within the G•7, caused a retrenchment in trade and business activity, which was badly needed for the emerging markets to facilitate the development of robust free markets. I believe that if Ronald Reagan were still President during the early 1990s, and the stimulus program that he instigated during the 1980s arms build-up was still a part of U.S. policy, the transition would be much easier for the former Soviet countries to adopt free market systems; leading to a faster level of prosperity for their citizens. This, however, did not happen, and the U.S. fell under the spell of tax increases by the Bush administration, leading to an unnecessarily severe recession.

Undoubtedly, the global economy combined with technological changes would have naturally resulted in a disinflationary climate for some members of the G•7, and a deflationary impact for others. There never seemed to be an offsetting policy by leading industrialised countries during these times, that would neutralise this natural tendency for lower levels of business activity. Consequently, shock therapy could have been more successful, if it had the support of more Reaganomics here. Instead, the lack of stimulus, combined with a policy of shock therapy, produced a spectacular increase in organised criminal activity and the rise of mafias. This explanation may be far too simplistic for many to comprehend, but the fall of Communism was an event which brought great puzzlement to most, in terms of the likely consequences for all prevailing interest groups within the G•7.

In addition, the movement towards independent central banking in countries that make up the newly-emerging markets, as well as those within the G•7 without such a tradition, also made matters worse. It was easy to comprehend, that inflation just is not, and never was a problem. Moreover, even in the latter half of the decade, inflation still was not a problem, which makes the stance by the Federal Reserve somewhat comical; if it were not so harmful. If the 1990s meant that a global market was in the process of construction, then the accession of a greater of supply of countries, hence products and commodities on offer, would need to be met by an equivalent increase in demand to ensure price stability. However, the financial system proved to be unbalanced, as supply emanating from countries such as Russia and Kazakhstan, was not being properly balanced off by policies that favoured greater aggregate global demand, leading to outcomes that were characterised by both disinflation as well as deflation.

Simply stated, now that Russia and all of the former Soviet countries were being tied into a global market, they were offering more oil, gas, wood, paper and minerals to traditional buyers around the world. The increase in supplies naturally cause prices to fall via the bidding process. The events in the early 1990s in the U.S., U.K. and Europe were not friendly, and did not help to facilitate these buyers of these traditional products, as both monetary and fiscal policies slowly began to retreat from the economic lives of companies and individuals everywhere. Moreover, the major arms spending build-up during the 1980s was over, and budget deficits needed to be covered at further costs to the robust development of this expanded global marketplace.

The lack of assistance in developing a robust connection to the G•7, exacerbated a breakdown in the effective functioning of free markets in countries such as Russia. Despite being resource rich, the deflationary climate globally was not friendly to profitable commodity sales. Among many other manufactured products, there was a transition issue in terms of the quality of what was being produced locally, but this was well recognized as such, and could not have been an excuse for the failure of an effective development of a market system in these countries during this period. After being "shocked" into the new market system, managers of the former state industries panicked, and the first thing to go domestically was the input supply-chain, which was artificially propped up by the Soviet government. The system was organised in an archaic way, with political factors playing the most important investment decisions of where to locate a particular plant, or even from where inputs would originate geographically in the productive process. A plant located in Moscow, may have been required by the Soviet government to order inputs from a plant in Siberia, despite the fact that a similar plant existed in Moscow. After there was no longer an authority capable of directing this type of system, and after the country opened to foreign opportunities, there was no reason to order inputs any longer from a plant that was based as far away as Siberia.

Moreover, the demand that was not centrally sponsored anymore by the Soviet government, for the outputs that this factory in Moscow was producing, now had to be sold through a form of promotion and marketing, not to mention advertising. Those managers that were not good at this form of corporate promotion, and the majority were not, needed to attract revenues for their enterprises to ensure that they were on-going concerns. Those who were the most unscrupulous, ran away with the companies treasury and crossed into Switzerland and Cyprus. However, for those who opted to stay, the game became very dangerous as survival of their livelihoods was foremost on their minds. They had to achieve revenues for their respective organisations at any cost, and were forced into organised bartering systems to ensure that inputs were forthcoming, as well as turning to strong-arm tactics against their suppliers. Unfortunately, there were many that began to associate the new global market system with outright robbery and thievery, against organisations and enterprises that continued to function normally and profitably during this period. Badly needed was hard currency through trade for many of these companies, so that they could ensure the continuity of their enterprises by engaging in foreign input purchases, if the supply broke down domestically. Unfortunately, the deflationary climate during this time among the G•7, did not facilitate this form of trade contact, which is the reason for the critique against the policies that were being pursued by both governments and central banks during this time.

In that respect, the rise of organised criminal activity was synonymous with the prevailing climate and lack of support externally, despite the move to implement a shock therapy policy, and also was a method of survival, given that managers and directors of the former state organisations had no experience in dealing with a situation where their output was forced to make a profit on its own, from the buying decisions of other businesses or consumers. In that sense, organised criminal activity was a surrogate for ignorance about the new system, and a general sense that the survival of these enterprises, was being deliberately threatened by the new government of Boris Yeltsin.

THE HARD TRANSITION TO GLOBAL TRANSPARENCY

The Cold War presented a fragmented pool of capital that was far more regional and country-specific than what globalisation presents today. Further, the main decision-making function for global capital flows has shifted from governments to private individuals, corporations and institutions. The enormous growth in productivity that technological change has made possible in the 1990s, has created more wealth than at any time in recent history. The breakdown of national barriers to capital flows continues, and financial markets are continuing to merge, creating the foundations for one common global equity market.

When the issue of transparency is raised, it is necessary to think of a two-speed global economy, consisting of an advanced industrialised grouping, formed around but not exclusive to the G•7, and those recently emerging market countries in central and eastern Europe, Asia and Latin America. The new power gained by private investors, consisting of individuals and organisations, requires that markets adopt a common international standard of checks and balances, if they hope to attract the massive pool of investable funds for projects based in their respective countries. This pool of capital has gained an unprecedented power to shape laws and political events in individual countries, as the U.K. government of John Major found out the hard way in 1992, with George Soros' instant notoriety over the breaking of the sterling peg to the Deutsche mark.

In essence, this event created by Soros was a signal to everyone that a new era was now in formation, one where the massive pool of capital that was building would have a lasting impact in promoting the concept of free markets. If any country among the emerging markets desired a standard of living that was world class, then it would need to tap into this massive global pool of capital with its proposals and projects. The necessary precondition for these new investors, however, would be the comfort of knowing that they would be able to pull out their investments, whenever better competing opportunities existed elsewhere in the world. This required laws that supported private property and supported the profit motive and shareholder value in stock markets and owner-ship stakes.

Most emerging countries have signalled to global investors, that they would like to join in this game of playing for a world class standard of living for their people. The only rogue states that currently stick out in my mind are Yugoslavia or Serbia under Slobodan Milosevic, and possibly North Korea, although recent moves to re-integrate with the south are beginning to show some promise. In addition, there are many countries in Africa and the Middle East, for instance, Iraq and Libya, that also are not interested in achieving western living standards and do not desire to enact policies that can attract for-eign investment.

Organised criminal activity in many newly-emerging countries, has replaced an efficient functioning of a free market, or has operated alongside some form of emerging free market. The process that will drive out uncertainties and close down these forms of black market activities, will be the only path for these countries to ensure that they will begin to compete effectively for the attention of legitimate global investors.

The growing power of globalisation is demanding more and more acts of trans-parency among all countries, including the G•7 themselves. The formerly parochial "old boys" clubs symbolised by the Stock Exchanges in Canada, have also been forced to change their ways. Throughout the year 2000, the Toronto Stock Exchange has one of the best performing indices in the world, attracting the attention of more foreign investors than ever before, after its executive moved very quickly to instill more transparency in relations with its listings and among its broker members. Recently, in conjunction with the Ontario Securities Commission (OSC), it charged one of the most "blue-chip" of Canadian banks, the Royal Bank, with stock manipulation charges punish-able by a fine and suspension of a group of high profile executives. The move surprised many long time practitioners, and solicited a public apology to its clients from CEO John Cleghorn, that was carried in every serious daily news-paper in Canada.

Likewise, the move towards fewer and fewer stock exchanges in the world has raised the stakes of transparency. What used to be a nightmare in coordination, among the many national stock markets, is fast becoming friendlier to foreign investment. The multitude of diverse trading systems and regulations for investors if they wanted to invest in Paris, as opposed to Amsterdam, is now becoming far less complex. Moreover, the combination of the London and Frankfurt or Stockholm stock exchanges, with the possibility of a link-up with the Nasdaq, will allow traders in any of these geographical locations to easily move capital between three or more vital financial centres in the world.

Financial market transparency is front and centre in the global environment today. However, there is a similar transparency that is also converging among countries that openly trade products in global markets. Very soon, not only China, but most of the emerging market countries will become members of the World Trade Organisation (WTO). National standards of individual countries will need to become globally standardised, as will the quality of products that hope to join the global market for goods as well as services. This area will lag the developments on the financial market side, since the ease of investing made possible by electronic technology, will force trade anomalies and barriers to come down eventually.

There will always be a formal and an informal sector that will operate side by side in virtually every country; to those that are not as yet predisposed to join-ing the club that is seeking a world standard of living. The formal sector will consist of the large corporate sector, to smaller and medium sized companies, that are meeting the common standards and are deemed as being "transparent." These will become candidates for attracting investment from the global pool of capital to finance their projects, expansions and merger and acquisition plans. By contrast, the informal sector will operate without adhering to such interna-tional standards, but will be operating perfectly legally by local standards. There will also be black market activity and organised crime that will never become plugged into the legitimate global system, and who will never particu-larly desire to participate in it. However, the trend is towards a greater global and transparent standard locally, among this diverse grouping of countries that desire to raise their living standards by using this massive pool of mobile investment capital.

Already, the transition towards transparency in emerging markets has initially affected their banking systems, as credit policy has been upgraded to coincide with the current standards within the G•7. Moreover, various forms of acquisi-tions and joint-ventures have exported a transparent approach to these countries which will be passed down to all local clients, demanding profitability, growth in revenues and positive cash-flows. If clients do not approve of this more rig-orous system, or they do not meet the standards, not only will they become iso-lated from the global pool of capital, but they will also experience difficulty in sustaining their local operations.

INTERNET AND HIGH TECH

The impact of technological change has always been difficult to predict. The former Soviet Union was largely based on asymmetries in information among the ruling elite and the governed. When the information based economy was still in its infancy in the early 1980s, cracks began to appear in the authority that the government usually relied on to ensure that order was preserved and that the system continued to function. I know from first hand experience, having made numerous excursions to the former Yugoslavia in the 1980s, just how the attitudes that favoured independence for many of the breakaway Republics gained an inertia of their own. As it became easier to organise an opposition via better and faster communications in the western countries, the ruling elite found the circumstances that developed more and more difficult to counter.

Likewise, as in the case of the large corporations and conglomerates, technological changes first witnessed in the early 1980s began to impact the way in which work was allocated. Many of these firms were not organised in accordance to profit-maximising activities, and many layers of middle management, or even administrative roles proved to be in severe overlap by the end of the decade. The financial sector has been the most susceptible to technology, and the innovations that have come on stream in terms of managing information and data, have immediately done away with several layers in their respective corporate structures. Moreover, competition and the greater ease of entry for competitors, has forced a flat structure in the banking and brokerage sectors, to ensure that client service is the most important mission in the firm; most employees have been forced to become marketers, often the only weapon in hand a small personal computer. Competition has become so intense, that many bankers and lawyers have begun making house calls in order to close their real estate transactions.

The rise of the internet has eliminated the traditional stock broker and the method in which he collects commissions on transactions. Now, companies such as E-Trade, Schwab and Ameritrade vie for the business of investors by offering very low fees on trades, with evidence of a handful of firms even offering free trading. This has caused a migration of knowledgeable stock market investors away from the traditional commission based full service brokerages, and has forced these firms to rewrite their business models.

The largest impact that technology and the internet have had is on the traditional menace of inflation. During the oil embargo years and the era of O.P.E.C. power in the 1970s, hyperinflation and stagflation became the conditions under which policy was directed in the form of Richard Nixon's wage and price controls. Soon thereafter, policy makers began proposing wildly speculative theories that the production process not only included labour and physical capital, but that a special consideration ought to be reserved for energy inputs. The 1970s were also a break with the traditional history of inflation, or its long term trend. For most of the preceding decades, inflation never proved to be a severe problem, except for in the 1970s.

Soon thereafter, many influential monetary economists such as Robert Barro, Robert Lucas and Thomas Sargent, began writing research papers that were widely read in the profession, and which became a lobbying cry for a transformation in the way in which central banks conduct monetary policy. The basic proposition stated that money supply expansions were directly linked to inflation, and that monetary policy was essentially useless in affecting economic growth if it were entirely anticipated by the public at large and by businesses. To put it concisely, monetary policy had no real effect on the economy or unemployment. This lobby cry was a direct evolution of the O.P.E.C. oil years of the 1970s, and began to reshape policy, just when technological changes and the internet naturally made such concepts as hyper-inflation and stagflation more or less redundant.

To be effective inflation fighters, central banks needed to be independent from political influence and accountable to no one. The German Bundesbank was the only institution of its kind that fit this criteria for most of the Cold War era, with the Federal Reserve having too much of an eclectic history for it to be labeled as being truly independent when it came to controlling inflation. The push was on to have all of the G•7 central banks become truly independent, and to have all of the European Union central banks independent, prior to the launch of the single European currency.

The road to independence gathered political and lobby strength in the 1990s, meanwhile the inflationary scare became less of a threat as the early signs of globalisation began to appear. The massive interconnection of markets into areas of the world that were formerly off-limits to free markets, exerted a tremendous psychological effect on consumers and producers; an effect that moved to wipe-out any lingering inflationary expectations carried over from the 1970s and the 1980s. There were no more bouts of hyper-inflation and wage and price controls were rarely mentioned in this new era. The impact of policy added to the difficulties which were experienced as a result of the sudden transformation from a Cold War economy, to one where there was now a massive free-for-all globally.

Logically, it would seem that monetary policy could move to offset the push of disinflation and outright deflation, creating a better balance for business, consumers and labour, not to mention emerging markets. This did not happen, and the deep transformation-induced depression of the early 1990s was deeper and harder than it may have been. Technology took over where the Berlin Wall effect ended, and ensured a continuation of the era of falling, or at best, stable prices. The prospect of an expanding internet economy by 1994, ensured that the overall climate of deflation would accelerate even further, holding prices at bay for possibly the remainder of the decade. Now that transactions costs were in a free-fall, it was very easy for buyers to compare the prices of a similar product online from a number of suppliers. What ensured that loyalty would continue to prevail in purchasing decisions under such heightened competitive conditions today? Many well respected strategists such as Warren Buffet of Berkshire Hathaway, openly came out and said that the new internet economy is a net destroyer of company values. The level of competition would be too destructive, and may immediately destroy the franchise values of some well-respected names in the marketplace. The transactions cost buffer could no longer be relied upon to deliver continued market power for those that are already firmly entrenched.

This newly competitive environment is rapidly spreading globally, and many leaders of the G•7 have come out publicly and stated that the internet is the only effective way in which under-developed countries in Africa can effectively join this new global economy. What is certain, is that inflation will not be an issue, and that our central banks will continue fighting a war that has already been won long ago.

GOODBYE FIFTY PERCENT!

The internet based global economy will have a far-reaching impact on many entrenched special interests, and will affect even those companies and industries that have come to dominate a particular market for centuries. A good case in point is the opaque art auction market, which has been traditionally controlled by a handful of centuries-old auctioneers. The best known have been Sotheby's and Christie's; both having British roots and actively involved in most major cities around the world.

An even more opaque market, has been the "living artist" market, or more commonly known as the contemporary art market, which is expected to be radically affected by the internet economy. Traditionally, there have been as little as three hundred living artists around the world, who could earn a "world-class" standard of living from the sales of their art work. Traditionally, there have also been specialised market-makers for this form of art; better known as "Gallerists," who operate a physical presentation space and ensure that a partic-

ular artist that they represent would generate sales in museums and private collections. This market is not transparent and usually carries a substantial transactions and entry cost. The transactions costs relate to the Gallerists building
up enough contacts that are interested in buying this art, both from the perspective of private collectors as well as museums, and those that relate to the costs
in searching for the appropriate artists to represent, hence understanding contemporary trends in terms of what art will sell and at what price?

The entry costs are enormous, since it takes Gallerists a very long time to
establish credibility when it comes to major museum clients that buy from
them, as well as the well known and marketable artists themselves who they
wish to represent. The Guggenheim Museum in New York will not simply buy
from anyone! All sales that Gallerists are able to generate from the artists that
they represent carry a commission charge of fifty percent. Meaning, that if a
work of art is sold by the Gallerist of German artist Gerhard Richter for one
million dollars to the Guggenheim Museum in New York, five hundred thousand is kept by the Gallerist as the commission in the transaction. How can the
development of the internet affect this process?

For one, a central web site will collect information about this segment of the
art world that was never available to collectors and museums before. The
artists themselves will be able to sell directly through the internet, and use an
auction system that is already developed on the internet via websites such as
e.bay. Well known names will be able to post a photo of the work, a description
along with the dimensions, and invite offers by interested buyers over a period
of one week to one month. The highest bidder wins, and the fifty percent normally transferred to the market-making Gallerists, can now be retained by the
artists themselves. The internet has immediately empowered the creators of art
and has cut out all of the middlemen in the process. This is a perfect example
of how an abstract market, functioning in an abstract system, can use the new
technology to create efficiencies, reduce transactions costs and become very
close to being transparent. Moreover, the market will retain its global character-
istics and even enhance them, as more and more internet users become more
familiar with this art form. In the end, just as the traditional stock broker
became redundant, so also may the Gallerist that does not find a way in which
to add substantial value to her or his commission charges. What may end up
happening in the end is that the old fifty percent rule could end up falling to ten
or twenty percent, making the Gallerist of value once again to the artist within
the new technological and information structure.

The same way in which an artist can become empowered in the new global
world of fast paced technology, so too can countries that are currently on the
fringe. The areas of the world that have been traditionally excluded from the
new global market could very well become players in the new age of informa-

tion and technology. The transactions costs associated with taking products through the inefficient distribution systems from Africa or eastern Europe, to the markets in the west, could be reduced once the middle-men are cut out of the picture entirely. Producers in these regions will be able to sell directly to the west and the large U.S. marketplace, hence benefitting from the new technology and communications infrastructure. It is no wonder that G•7 leaders and Russia have come out in favour of accelerating the communications revolution in these parts of the world, as being the most effective way in which they can climb out of their development challenges of the past.

A major impact of the information economy will also come to affect the automotive sector in a big way. Traditionally, cars have been sold via a dealer network that used very aggressive "push" techniques in moving the inventory off of the lot. The "Big 3" U.S. automakers were often criticised by consumers for the aggressive and underhanded sales techniques that these salespeople employed. Further, many consumers that needed a new car, deliberately held off the purchase of a new one, for the sole reason that they did not enjoy going into a dealership environment. Enter the internet, and a radical new way of selling cars. What was at one time characterised as a "push" driven industry at the retail level, will eventually become a "pull" oriented industry on the internet. Consumers will increase their choices, by not being pressured to sign for a deal at a dealership, yet win some time in the comforts of their own homes in building the car with the options that they really want. Already, Ford Motor Company has aggressively adopted this framework, much to the disappointment of its dealer network, which have gone as far as challenging the emerging distribution system through the legal system in Canada.

Likewise, the market for used vehicles has also become more transparent with the new technology. What used to be one of the most dissatisfying consumer experiences; the act of buying a used car, has all of a sudden become more civil through the internet. Instead of having as many different quotes for a 1995 Honda Civic, as there were used car vendors, now various websites dedicated to used car sales come with a list price that allows the buyer to compare each offer by the stroke of a mouse click. Cars that are not reasonably priced on the internet simply will not move, while those that are priced attractively will receive a number of attractive offers. Both the new and used car sectors have been undergoing a revolution in marketing as a result of the new technology.

The most dramatic development with the internet has been its embrace by the more traditional industries. Recently, the procurement activities of a number of important sectors have been aggregated under a centralised buying portal. For example, Chicago based Sears department store in the U.S. has opened all of its procurement buying wide open to suppliers that make bids via the internet portal. Likewise, the U.S. airline industry has created such a system for its procurement practices, as have numerous other industrial sectors. This has raised concerns from the Federal Trade Commission (FTC), responsible for anti-trust activities to take a very careful look at the trend that has been developing recently. The creation of an industry-wide portal can create an environment that enhances competitiveness, and most of them have been designed specifically for this reason, however, there may also exist situations where collusion between the participants within a sector arise.

The problems of the economies of scale that are achieved by individual suppliers is a major factor, since a large supplier is able to expand production at a far lower cost, than is a supplier that is half its size. If the airline sector is advertising for new bids for an inventory of tires for the next year, then the largest company will be able to meet the demands of all U.S. airlines on the internet portal for tires at a fraction of the cost of its next competitor, that may be half its size, but with a far higher cost base for meeting the large order. The FTC has promised to watch for collusion among the participants on both sides on such internet portals, in their procurement practices from here on.

LONG TERM STRATEGIES

The progress from the Cold War to globalisation has reallocated savings from bank accounts and risk-free bonds to stocks. This is based more on expectations of spectacular returns, than it is on the evidence of real long term returns on risk-free bonds relative to equities. If we consider the long term fifty year real yield averages of stocks in New York, by taking the statistical evidence from the S&P500 real earnings and the S&P 500 real dividends, and comparing this to the real yields on risk-free bonds; both the short 91 day treasury bill and the long bond, stock returns are ahead of the bonds, but not by much.

An approximate calculation shows that the real yield on S&P500 earnings is approximately 3.4 percent over the past fifty year time horizon, but that the other measure of returns on stocks, the real dividend yield over this same period is the worst performer at approximately negative 0.2 percent. Therefore, the overall real yield on stocks as measured by the earnings component and the dividend component is approximately 3.2 percent. In relation to the real yields on both short and long term risk-free treasury bonds, the S&P500 still outperforms over a fifty year time frame, which takes into consideration all structural events such as the 1970s oil embargo and the power of O.P.E.C.; the Cold War era and the accession of the high interest rate strategy in 1981 by the Paul Volcker Federal Reserve, including the 1990s era of globalisation and rapid technological change.

Taking the time frame from 1981 onwards, the yield on the long treasury bond is the best, with the real yield on the 91 day treasury bill and the real yield on the S&P500 virtually similar, but lower than that of the long bond. Again, the real yield on the S&P dividends is at the bottom and not a serious consideration for investors. It is clear that ever since the Federal Reserve under Paul Volcker in 1981 adopted monetary targeting, and a conscious decision to keep inflation under control, the long bond has been the greatest beneficiary.

Taking a different time frame from the collapse of the Cold War in 1991 to the decade of globalisation in the 1990s, reveals the same evidence as the time frame from 1981, with one exception. The long bond real yield is still the best performer in the deflationary, or to a lesser degree disinflationary 1990s, with a marginal improvement in the 90 day treasury bill compared to its trend in the 1980s. However, what is interesting here is that the real yield on dividends is still not a factor and remains marginally negative, but the performance of the S&P500 earnings component seems to have peaked around the middle of the decade at about 1995, and has since fallen back to where it was in the early years of the 1990s. Given that the evidence for real earnings is on a downswing in the latter half of the 1990s, what then can account for the record rise in stock market indices during this period?

For one, the S&P500 benchmark may not adequately take into consideration a high technology component such as is available through the Nasdaq index. Also, the recent upward rise in stocks can be justified based on future expected productivity gains and expected earnings over a longer time frame. Moreover, if growth is taken into consideration, the internet and the high tech stocks are at the leading edge of spectacular earnings surges. Given all of these considerations, stocks could be fully justified for moving upwards, despite the evidence that real yields on S&P500 earnings is declining.

The fact that the long Treasury bond has outperformed over the 1990s should not be very surprising, given that fixed income investments that are safe, typically do very well during times of deflation or disinflation, as was the case in the early years of the decade. The earnings component of the S&P500 measure and the fact that real yields have been falling is an indication of the rapid real increase in the prices of equities. The unprecedented wealth effect that was made available from the productivity gains in the U.S. and the structural change that has favoured stock market investing in the 1990s, can account for the rapid increase. In short, the crude explanation is that there is just so much money in the latter half of the 1990s, chasing so few traditional assets with marginally acceptable returns. Even the gauge in the informal small and medium sized acquisitions market; the actual buying and selling of privately held, non-listed companies, shows incredible multiples that are being offered for generators of positive cash-flows and profitability. What used to be a market that had four to five bidders for every seller in the early part of the 1990s, ended up with as many as twenty to fourty buyers, depending on the industry. It remains very difficult to acquire an attractive asset with a solid cash-flow, given the climate of too few investment opportunities and so much money that exists today.

What will be the next investment trend that will yield an above average rate of return for investors? From the perspective of portfolio investors, the most conservative strategies that preferred a heavy weighting in risk-free treasury bonds, benefitted the most in the latter decade of the Cold War; the 1980s. A plentiful supply of high nominal rate bonds were made available, together with the hyper-inflation decade of the 1970s coming to an end. The real gains on offer during this time were very generous in retrospect, given that inflation was on the decline and real returns on the way up. The bond investors of the 1980s needed to shift strategies in the deflationary 1990s, as real returns were stable, but rates of return in no way could be compared to the capital gains that were evident in blue-chip stocks. At the height of the trough in the early 1990s, when the process of transformation from a Cold War economy to globalisation was in full swing, it was believed by many that stocks would not become such a natural destination for capital flows, but that cheap real-estate and commercial property could see some sort of resurgence. This did not happen, and as interest rates fell further, stock markets began their spectacular move upwards.

As the Dow Jones Industrial Average surpassed the 5,000 level, many respected analysts and investors began to call for a "crash." This also did not happen as yet, and the decade of the 1990s remained to be "crash-less," while the massive increase of wealth during this time enabled many ventures in high tech and the internet to flourish. The general condition whereby budget surpluses in the G•7 caused bond redemptions, adjusted many diversified portfolios to hold a sixty percent weighting in equities and a fourty percent weighting in bonds, whereas the Cold War allocation was usually the reverse of this.

If investors missed the early calling to stocks in the 1990s, many refused to join later on when the bull market was gaining momentum, for they feared getting caught in some kind of market correction that could sustain losses for a very long time. This also did not happen yet, except for a few scares along the way, and especially in 1998, when the Federal Reserve moved to bail-out Long Term Capital Management and the Russians defaulted on their bonds. The "structural" change had occurred; globalisation has dawned on us, and if you were not a participant in the bull stock market, you missed the boat. This, however, is now history, and a good long term strategist will begin to look for the next signs of some sort of structural change that could reverse these record equity markets, and create a new opportunity once again. This is not easy to predict, after all no one is always right; not even George Soros. Developments that are of interest, however, could be related to one or more of the following "structural" ideas:

More yen bonds

The fact that the Japanese yen denominated bond market will overtake the size of the U.S. Treasury bond market, given the deficit financing requirement of Japan and the countless stimulus programs that they felt obliged to implement. Institutional investors will begin to add this yen denominated risk-free supply of debt to their portfolios, hence raising the demand for yen in global global currency markets, despite the on-going depression domestically.

Euro Behind Record M&A

Armed with a new Euro that is supported by a very deep capital market and a growing global currency market, European conglomerates and corporations will continue to buy U.S. based assets at astronomical prices. This time around they will have the large Euro markets behind them, and be able to use the new deeper and bigger domestic capital markets to fund these ventures.

U.S. Corporations Revisit Europe

U.S. companies will begin to look at continental Europe more favourably, and will begin to re-allocate some commitments made in the U.K. which are being adversely affected by the strong level of the pound sterling.

Canadian Diversification Attractive Globally

Canada could become a favourite destination for foreign investors, given the fact that some leading high tech brands are based there and that it will continue to have its traditional resource base intact. A combination of Nortel Networks and Falconbridge could be irresistible to many foreign investors in terms of forming a natural diversification strategy.

Bond Scarcity

Both stocks and U.S. bonds will continue to yield equivalent returns with bond prices naturally pushed higher as the national debt is slowly wiped out.

"0" Interest Rates

With less funds committed to funding the national debt and deficits investors will find it hard to achieve increasing returns with low levels of risk, which may result in other G·7 countries going the direction of Japan and having interest rates just marginally positive.

Capital Ideas

Less government demand for capital will allow more idea-driven financing as more and more venture capital funds are set up and ideas that are beyond high tech begin to attract their fair share of capital.

Easy Capital for Small Companies with Track Records

Companies that have been in business for more than a year and are profitable whether small or large, will find it easy to attract financing at reasonable interest rates.

Small Company M&A Bids Supported

Smaller companies will begin to gain the support of bankers in their drive to enter the market for acquisitions.

Savings Shift

Investors will begin to by-pass traditional banks and seek out alternative asset classes that are showing respectable yields.

Art Market Transparency

Investments such as contemporary art that is internationally recognised will gain a level of transparency and attract even more investors' attention as an acceptable form of investment and store of value raising the prices of existing collections and making a market for works that were once considered as being hard to sell.

Efficient Markets

Just as in the case of contemporary art or antiques, all markets that were once characterised as being imperfect and containing very high transactions costs and asymmetrical information will begin to approach efficiencies and transparency.

Japan Slowest to "Globalise"

Japanese culture and customs will continue to conflict with globalisation causing a prolonged period of recession and sub-optimal performance.

Venture Exchanges to Rise

The market capitalisation value of venture capital markets like the Neuer Markt in Germany and the Canadian venture exchange may exceed the values of the major blue-chip markets and Nasdaq in New York over the long term.

One Global Stock Exchange Open 24 Hours

There will be one global stock exchange with one common legal basis and regulatory structure with twenty-four hour trading.

One Global Anti-Trust Regulator

There will be a global anti-trust agency set up that will equal the scope of the

World Trade Organisation (WTO) as cross border mergers and acquisitions become more common and a part of the daily news headlines.

Corporations Continue to Overpower Governments
Private corporations will continue to surpass the power of governments.

Inflation is Dead
Inflation will only occur temporarily and mainly because of scarcity eliminating the phenomenon of monetary inflation. The internet will encourage quick and easy "comparison shopping" even though sales will continue to account for a fraction of overall GDP.

Too Many Investment Funds
There will be too many investment and pension funds chasing too few good "mainstream" opportunities.

Real Investments Better than Financial
Savings will achieve better returns if invested in real productive ideas and assets than they will if they are in stocks and bonds.

"Risk Averse" Investors Forced to Take Risk
Risk-free investors will continue to face a rate of return dilemma.

New Role for Central Banks Needed
Central banks will turn their attentions away from fighting inflation and towards regulating global capital flow risks.

Emerging Markets Will Always be Enticing
Emerging market investments will become the "only game in town" for investors seeking an adequate return along with traditional "high-yield" bonds.

Death of the Business Cycle
Boom-bust cycles will be no more or barely noticeable. Rising economic activity will be supported by massive money and credit supply increases as was evidenced throughout 1995 and the summer of 2000, when a severe "overshoot" in venture capital equity investments unleashed an unprecedented "feel good" factor in the U.S.

Population Growth to Rise with Technology
Technological advancements will offset the real economic effects of population growth via advancements in agricultural technologies and biotechnology.

End of Monetary and Fiscal Policies
Monetary and fiscal policies will retreat in importance creating the conditions for rapid growth in business activity.

Wealth to be Uneven Globally
Distribution of rising wealth will become a primary issue.

Stock Market Listings to be Exclusively High Tech
Lack of investor interest will prompt "old economy" industries to de-list their under-valued stocks.

A Downturn in High Tech Will Exacerbate Investor's Paradox
Any setback or downturn in internet and high technology stocks or any correction in the current "dot.com" and high tech and telecoms economies will be met by aggressive interest rate cuts by the Fed, re-visiting the recessionary climate in the early to mid 1990s. Despite the deflating high tech "bubble," there will still be too much money available with very little scope of achieving reasonable returns on risk-free investments. Old economy small and mid-sized companies demonstrating solid cash-flows will see their value premiums rise exponentially, repeating the conditions existing between 1992 and 1995.

These are some of the "structural" events that can occur individually, or can combine with one another and exert a multi-dimensional effect on our three investment stories; global portfolio investment; foreign direct investment and cross border mergers and acquisitions. Needless to say, structural changes in business conditions and in the economy, has been a central theme of *The G•7 Report Project* throughout the rapid progression of the globalisation decade of the 1990s. What follows in this publishing program with the four related books *(I: THREE INVESTMENT STORIES UNDER FREE TRADE: Portfolio, Direct and Cross Border M&A; II: Political, Structural and Technological Change; III: Emerging Markets and Special Surveys; IV: Organised Crime and Money Laundering)* is an archive of articles that were published in *The G•7 Report's* Newsmagazine between 1992 and 1999, the most inciteful of which we are reproducing in this set. I hope that this series of books in its entirety, will come to serve as a primary account and authority of the business and economic history of this most revolutionary of decades in recent memory. In this respect, I hope that everyone will be able to effectively use this series of books as a vital reference, and also enjoy and be entertained by it.

William B.Z. Vukson
Toronto, Canada

PHOTO GALLERY

Top left and right: Bank of France
Executive, Jean-Claude Trichet (third from
right) future President of the European
Central Bank

Bottom left: Bruxelles Bourse

Bottom right: Bank of France

Top left: National Bank of Croatia

Top right: Bugatti EB 18/4 "Veyron". Auto industry moves to high tech in performance and design.

Bottom left: Nautilus by Pininfarina

Bottom right: Gianni Agnelli, Chairman of Fiat Group.

Printed by Printcorp LP № 347 of 11.05.99. Kuprevich St., 18, 220141, Belarus.
Ord. 0122A. Qty 1 050 cps.